Jane W. Buckingham

The Housekeeper's Friend

A practical cook-book

Jane W. Buckingham

The Housekeeper's Friend
A practical cook-book

ISBN/EAN: 9783744788991

Printed in Europe, USA, Canada, Australia, Japan

Cover: Foto ©Lupo / pixelio.de

More available books at **www.hansebooks.com**

THE HOUSEKEEPER'S FRIEND:

A Practical Cook-Book,

COMPILED BY

A LADY OF ZANESVILLE,

AND SOLD FOR THE

Benefit of the Home of the Friendless.

"Behold! his breakfasts shine with reputation;
His dinners are the wonder of the nation!
With these he treats both commoners and quality,
Who praise, where'er they go, his hospitality."

"All human history attests
That happiness for man—the hungry sinner—
Since Eve ate apples, must depend on dinner."

ZANESVILLE, OHIO:
SULLIVAN & PARSONS, PRINTERS AND BINDERS, 87 MAIN STREET.
1876.

Entered according to Act of Congress, in the year 1876, by J. W. B., in the Office of the Librarian of Congress at Washington, D. C.

PREFACE.

THIS book is entirely practical — nothing else. It contains no theoretic dissertation on the culinary art, but is made up of receipts which have been kindly sent me by my friends, and thoroughly tested by them; also many which have been my daily assistance for nineteen years in the management of my house, and the preparation of various dishes served for large and small companies.

The proceeds of the book will be devoted to the "Home of the Friendless," of Zanesville, Ohio, an institution most worthy of the patronage of all *benevolent people.*

Hoping the work will find favor in the eyes of the public (if not for its own merits) for the noble cause it represents, I leave it with them, and ask their patronage and sympathy.

J. W. B.

Zanesville, January, 1876.

MEASURES.

FROM ST. LOUIS COOK BOOK.

Wheat Flour,......................................one pound is one quart.
Indian Meal,....................... ......one pound, two ounces is one quart.
Butter when soft,............................ ......one pound is one quart.
Loaf Sugar, broken,..............................one pound is one quart.
White Sugar, powdered,...........one pound, one ounce is one quart.
Best Brown Sugar,........ ....one pound, two ounces is one quart.
Ten Eggs,................ .... are one quart.
Flour, ...four pecks are one bushel.
Sixteen large teaspoonfuls,...................... ....are one pint.
Eight large teaspoonfuls,........ ....are one gill.
Four large teaspoonfuls,..are $\frac{1}{2}$ gill.
A common size tumbler,...is $\frac{1}{2}$ pint.
A common size wine glass,....................................is $\frac{1}{2}$ gill.
A tea-cup,................. ....is one gill.
A large wine glass, ...is one gill.
A large tablespoonful,................. ....is $\frac{1}{2}$ ounce.
Forty drops equal to. ....one teaspoonful.
Four teaspoonfuls equal to............................one tablespoonful.

DINNER BILL OF FARE.

FIRST COURSE.—Raw oysters, or raw clams with lemon.
SECOND COURSE.—Soup, if two kinds, one light and the other dark.
THIRD COURSE.—Fish, if two kinds, one boiled and the other baked, with cucumber salad.
FOURTH COURSE.—Roast meats, with two or three vegetables, and celery.
FIFTH COURSE.—Game or chicken; salad and currant jelly.
SIXTH COURSE.—Pie or pudding.
SEVENTH COURSE.—Ice-cream, jelly, cake, Charlotte Russe, &c., &c.
EIGHTH COURSE.—Fruit.
NINTH COURSE.—Bon-bons, dried fruits, nuts.
TENTH COURSE.—Coffee.
Asparagus or cauliflower make a very nice course, between the meat and game course.

COMBINATIONS.

Mutton chops and tomato sauce are good together.
Roast mutton, currant jelly and turnips.
Venison and currant jelly.
Any kind of game, and currant jelly.
Any kind of game and salad.
Fish and cucumbers.
Raw oysters and lemon.
Roast goose and apple sauce.
Roast duck and apple sauce.
Turkey and cranberry sauce.
Fried oysters and salad.
Onions with all kinds of poultry.
Lamb and peas.
Salmon and peas.
Sweet-breads and tomatoes.
Boiled mutton and caper sauce, turnips.
Roast lamb and mint sauce.
Cresses with chicken.
Tomatoes are nice with anything.

THE HOUSEKEEPER'S FRIEND.

SOUPS.

VEGETABLE SOUP.

Put a pint of Lima beans, a half dozen large tomatoes, two teacupfuls of dried corn, or corn cut from the cob, a few snap-beans, and two teaspoonfuls of dried ochra into five quarts of water, with three slices of lean ham. Boil for two hours, and season with salt and pepper. Remove the ham before sending to table. Thicken with yellow of egg and a little flour. A nice winter soup is made by boiling a few slices of lean ham, half a pint of dried Lima beans, a few heads of celery cut up, and turnips and potatoes sliced thin. A fourth of a teacupful of dried ochra will be a nice addition, and a grated carrot, or half a teacupful of stewed tomatoes, preserved in cans, will improve the color. If thickening is required add some made of browned flour and water. Two tablespoonfuls of pepper-sauce will improve it. Put it in after it is in the tureen.

OYSTER SOUP. (Without Oysters.)

MRS. HERRON, CINCINNATI.

Boil one and a half dozen onions in water enough to cover them; if the onions are small take two dozen, if strong, boil a turnip with them which will destroy the strong taste. When they are soft enough, mash them very smooth through a colander, then boil them again in one quart of milk. Mix one teaspoonful of flour with one tablespoonful of butter, and stir in the soup. Let it boil up thoroughly and season with pepper, salt, and mace.

PEA SOUP.

Soak a quart of split peas in cold water over night. Then put them into a pot with two gallons of water, six cold boiled potatoes, two onions well sliced, one pound of pork or an old ham-bone or one pound of dried beef. Cover very closely; boil very slowly for five hours. Season to the taste with pepper and salt. One tablespoonful of celery seed imparts a fine flavor. Serve the pork on a platter with vegetables after the soup.

TOMATO SOUP. (No. 1.)
MRS. HERRON, CINCINNATI.

Take two quarts of tomatoes, one small marrow bone, one cucumber, one onion, six ochras, and three pints of water. Wash the tomatoes, scald the water, scald the tomatoes in it, and then use it for the soup. Rub the tomatoes through a colander. Boil all the materials three hours, stirring frequently. When it begins to thicken add boiling water until it becomes the right consistency. Just before it is done add one teaspoonful of flour. Season with cayenne pepper and salt.

TOMATO SOUP. (No. 2.)

Cook thoroughly, as for canning, some tomatoes, about one quart after they are cooked, season with pepper, salt and butter. Then pour into a large tureen three pints of boiling milk; stir in together a teaspoonful of soda, dissolved in a small quantity of cold milk, and the tomatoes. These should be stirred in simultaneously with the soda. Add some rolled crackers, and serve immediately. This is equal to oyster soup.

OYSTER SOUP.

Strain the liquor from two quarts of oysters, add to it an equal quantity of water. Put it on to boil, and skim it. Then throw in a little white pepper, a head of celery cut in small pieces, and a third of a pound of butter, with two teaspoonfuls of flour rubbed in it. Boil it five minutes longer, and put in the oysters, and a pint of cream, and after one more boil pour into the tureen, in which have some toasted bread cut in small pieces, and a little finely cut parsley.

To Prepare a Beef's Head as Stock for Soup.

Cut up the head into small pieces, and boil in a large quantity of water until it is boiled all to pieces. Take out all the bones, as in making cheese souse, and boil again until thick. Then season very highly with pepper, salt, catsup, allspice, and onions chopped fine. Place in a crock or jar, and set away for future use. For a small family cut out a thick slice, (say five inches square,) whenever you want soup in a hurry, and add about one quart of boiling water. It need cook for a few minutes only, and is valuable as keeping well, and being ready for times of emergency. By the addition of a few sliced hard-boiled eggs, and a gill of good cooking wine, this soup may have very nearly the flavor of mock-turtle.

VERMICELLI SOUP.
DIXIE COOK BOOK.

Put four pounds of any kind of fresh meat, except pork, into a gallon of cold water, cover close, and boil gently until the meat is tender. Throw in a head of celery, and half an hour afterwards take it from the fire, strain and return it to the pot. Season with salt and pepper. Add vermicelli, which has been scalded in boiling water in the proportion of four ounces to two quarts of soup. Let it boil ten minutes, and pour into the tureen.

NOODLE SOUP

Is made in the same way, except that strips of paste are substituted for the vermicelli. The paste is prepared by beating three eggs very light, and making them into a stiff dough with flour and water. They are then kneaded well and rolled very thin, cut into fine narrow strips, and dried a short time on dishes in the sun or oven; if you do this they must be soaked a short time before putting them in the soup, but I often put them in without drying. They will require to be boiled a little longer than vermicelli.

RICH WHITE SOUP.

MRS. J. FULTON.

Take a pair of large fat fowls and cut them up. Butter the soup pot and put in the pieces, with two pounds of the lean of veal cut in pieces. Season with one-half teaspoonful of salt, same of cayenne pepper and mace, cover with water and stew slowly for an hour, skimming it well. Then take out the breasts and wings of the fowls and chop the meat fine, leaving the rest stewing. Mix the chopped chicken with the grated crumbs of a quarter of a loaf of stale bread, having soaked the crumbs in a little warm milk. Have ready the yolks of four hard-boiled eggs, one dozen sweet almonds and six bitter ones, blanched and broken small. Mix eggs, almonds, chicken, and bread, pound well in a mortar, strain the soup from the meat and fowl, and stir this mixture in after it is reduced to two quarts. Boil separately one quart of cream or rich milk, and add it hot to the soup a little at a time, and let it simmer a few minutes longer.

RICH BROWN SOUP.

MRS. J. FULTON.

Take six pounds of lean fresh beef, cut from the bone. Stick over it four dozen cloves. Season it with one teaspoonful of salt, one teaspoonful of pepper, same of mace and nutmegs; (onions;) Pour on five quarts of water and stew slowly five or six hours, skimming well. When the meat is in shreds, strain it, and return the liquid to the pot, then add a tumbler and a half of claret or port wine. Simmer it slowly until dinner time or until reduced to three quarts.

CHICKEN SOUP.

Cut up two chickens, and put them in a pot with five quarts of cold water. Season with salt and pepper. Let them boil until the meat is very well done, and remove it from the liquor, and cut it up into small pieces. Put in the soup a quarter of a pound of butter mixed with a little flour, and a pint of cream. Throw in the cut meat, and just before you serve it add the beaten yolks of two eggs, and a little parsley. You may also add (if in season) a pint of green corn cut from the cob, and put in when it is half done. Squirrel soup is made in the same way.

FISH.

TO BAKE A SHAD, OR WHITE FISH.

Prepare a stuffing of bread crumbs, salt, pepper, butter, and a little parsley, mix it up with the beaten yolk of two or three eggs, according to the quantity of stuffing required; fill the fish with it, and tie a string firmly about it. Pour over it a little water, and some butter, and bake as you would a fowl. A shad will require from an hour to an hour and a quarter to bake. White fish not quite as long. Rock fish is baked in the same way, but requires a longer time to cook.

TO BOIL SALT SHAD OR MACKEREL.

DIXIE COOK BOOK.

If very salt, the fish must be soaked twelve hours in plenty of cold water. Or if the water is changed, a shorter time will be required. Put it into a skillet or frying-pan, with cold water enough to cover it, and let it boil fifteen minutes. Then change the water for fresh hot water, and after boiling in this fifteen minutes longer, take it up, and serve with drawn butter, and garnish with parsley. Another nice way to dress salt fish, is to boil together for ten minutes a tea-cup of cream, some cut parsley, and a little butter and pepper, and if the cream is not very thick, a beaten yolk of an egg, and pour it over the fish when it is ready to send to the table.

FRIED OYTSERS.

Make a batter of the yellow of egg, flour, and a little water. Roll some cracker very fine, and after wiping the oysters, dip first into the batter, and then into the cracker. Fry them in half lard and half butter, till a rich brown.

SCALLOPED OYSTERS.

Fill a buttered dish with alternate layers of oysters and grated bread-crumbs, pepper, butter, and salt, (a piece of mace to each layer is an addition,) have a thick layer of crumbs on top. Place in a moderately heated oven, and bake fully an hour. When it commences to brown on top, place a paper over it, and allow to bake thoroughly through, then remove the paper, and brown to a rich color on top. No oyster liquor need be put in, as there will be enough when they are cooked.

OYSTER PIE.

Strain the liquor from the oysters, and put it on to boil with butter, and pepper, and a thickening of bread-crumbs and milk well beaten together, and after boiling a few minutes, throw in the oysters. Let them remain five minutes, take them off, and when warm add the beaten yolks of three eggs. Line a buttered dish with a paste, and fill with white paper or a clean napkin, to support a lid of paste, and bake it. When lightly browned, take off the lid, remove the napkin, pour in the oysters, set a few minutes in the oven, and send to table hot.

SPICED OYSTERS.

MRS. J. FULTON.

Pick over and wash the oysters, strain the liquor, and pour it over the oysters again. Then put over the fire with cloves, mace and pepper, and let them come to a boil, then skim them. When quite cool, add enough vinegar to suit your taste, and slice a lemon into it.

SCRAMBLED OYSTERS.

MRS. MERSHON.

Put your oysters in a colander, and allow all the liquor to run through. Into this liquor put a lump of butter about as large as a walnut, some pepper and salt. Put it on the stove and let it get thoroughly hot, then put your oysters into it. Have ready some bread nicely toasted, place it on a flat dish, and when the oysters are thoroughly cooked pour them over the toast.

COD FISH BALLS.

Take cod-fish either salt or fresh, that has been boiled; remove the bones carefully and mince the fish; mix with it some mashed potatoes, one-third cod-fish and two-thirds potatoes, season with butter and pepper, and mix all together until quite smooth; if it seems dry moisten with a little cream or milk, or the beaten yolk of an egg. Make into small cakes, sprinkle with flour, and fry in hot lard to a nice brown. Send to table hot.

EGGS.

OMELET. (Delicious.)

MRS. SILVEY.

Eight eggs, one tea-cup of sweet milk, one tablespoonful of flour, one tablespoonful of melted butter. Beat the whites of four of the eggs separately, beat the yolks of the eggs very light, mix in the other ingredients, then pour into a frying-pan with a small quantity of butter; as it stiffens put the whites over it, cut into slices, and roll over and over with a broad knife, salt and pepper as you turn it. Put only about a third of the yolk into the pan at a time, also reserving the same quantity of the whites, so as to send into the table several times hot.

OMELET. (No. 2.)

MRS. HERRON, CINCINNATI.

Seven eggs beaten separately. To the yolks add one-half tea-cup milk, two small tablespoonfuls of flour, one teaspoonful of salt, then add the whites after they have been beaten light. Place in a skillet or frying-pan, one cup of butter; after it becomes hot, pour in some of the mixture, let it brown, and then fold over, and work in a trifle more. It should be quite brown on the outside, and soft in the middle.

OMELET. (No. 3.)

Take three tablespoonfuls of milk for each egg, a pinch of salt to each one also, beat the eggs lightly for three or four minutes, and pour them into a hot pan, in which a piece of butter the size of a walnut has been melted a moment before. The mass will begin to bubble, and rise in flakes immediately, and the bottom must be lifted incessantly with a knife, to allow the softer part to run in. An omelet should be cooked about three or four minutes, and made in this way will melt in the mouth.

SCRAMBLED EGGS.

Melt a tablespoonful of butter in a saucepan; beat the yolks of six eggs a few minutes, then add to them six tablespoonfuls of milk, and a teaspoonful of salt, beat a little longer, and pour them into the melted butter. When they thicken slightly, pour in the whites unbeaten, and mix them with the yolks carefully with a fork. Serve on pieces of toast in a hot dish, or if preferred omit the toast. The whites should not be beaten in hard, only stirred with the fork enough to mix slightly with the rest.

SCRAMBLED EGGS. (A More Simple Way.)

Beat six or eight eggs very light, add a little salt, and put into a warm frying-pan with a small quantity of butter. Stir them until they are well thickened, but not hard; sprinkle a little pepper over them, and send to table in a hot dish.

OMELET.

MRS. B. WHEELER.

Five eggs, one-half cup of milk, one tablespoonful of flour, a little salt. Break the eggs separately, whites on a plate and yolks in a bowl. Beat each thoroughly, and stir the milk and flour with the yolks. Have your skillet very hot, and buttered well, turn half the yolks into it, and spread half the beaten whites on top. It will brown in a moment, then roll over and over as you would a jelly-cake roll.

SAUCES.
(FOR MEATS.)

DRAWN BUTTER.

Mix together, one quarter of a pound of butter, and one tablespoonful of flour. Put one pint of water into a kettle, and when it boils, stir in the flour, and butter, Season with salt, and white pepper, and celery if in season, removing the stalks of celery before sending to the table. It will require but a few minutes boiling, and must be stirred constantly.

EGG SAUCE

Is made as drawn butter, with the addition of six hard boiled eggs cut in small pieces, and stirred in a few minutes before removing from the fire. This sauce is usually served with fish.

MINT SAUCE.

Take the leaves of young mint, and cut up finely, and to three tablespoonfuls of chopped mint add one of sugar, and vinegar sufficient to moisten the mint, and sugar well. Put in a little salt, and serve with roast lamb.

YORKSHIRE PUDDING. (To eat with Roast Beef.)

MRS. QUETTING OF BROOKLYN.

One pint of milk, two eggs well beaten, a little salt, and flour to make a batter half as thick as for pan cakes. Bake in the fat of the meat, and eat with the beef gravy. Place it on the dish under the beef when you serve it.

CELERY SAUCE.

Cut up a large bunch of celery into small pieces. Use only that which is blanched, throw aside the green tops. Put it into a pint of water and boil until it is tender. Then add a teaspoonful of flour, and a lump of butter the size of an egg, mixed well together. Season with salt and white pepper, and stir constantly until removed from the fire. It is nice with boiled poultry.

SALADS.

A RECEIPT FOR SALAD.

SIDNEY SMITH.

To make this condiment your poet begs,
The pounded yellow of two hard-boiled eggs;
Two boiled potatoes, passed through kitchen sieve,
Smoothness and softness to the salad give;
Let onion atoms lurk within the bowl,
And, half suspected, animate the whole;
Of mordant mustard add a single spoon,
Distrust the condiment that bites so soon;
But deem it not, thou man of herbs, a fault
To add a double quantity of salt;
Four times the spoon with oil from Lucca crown,
And twice with vinegar, procured from town;

And lastly, o'er the flavored compound toss
A magic soupçon of anchovy sauce.
O green and glorious! O herbaceous treat!
'T would tempt the dying anchorite to eat;
Back to the world he'd turn his fleeting soul,
And plunge his fingers in the salad-bowl;
Serenely full, the epicure would say,
"Fate cannot harm me,—I have dined to-day."

Chicken Salad. (For Four Chickens.)
MRS. GRANT, PHILADELPHIA.

The yolks of ten hard boiled eggs, the yolks of three raw eggs, one small teaspoonful of fine salt, one-half teaspoonful of cayenne pepper, one and a half tablespoonfuls of mustard mixed with a little vinegar, one tea-cup of vinegar, one-half bottle of the best salad oil. Process: Break the yolks of three eggs into a deep dish, add the mustard, mix it well, drop the oil in, stirring all the time. Then take yolks of the ten hard boiled eggs, mash them up fine, mixing in the salt, pepper and vinegar. Let this second dressing be lightly stirred into the first. Then season the chickens with pepper and salt, cut them up fine, and add the celery. Mix the dressing well through it leaving enough of the celery tops to garnish the dish for the table. The celery should be nicely cleansed, cut fine, and put to soak in cold water until wanted, then turn on a cloth, and wipe it quite dry. Have about as much celery as chicken.

CHICKEN SALAD.

Boil two (or if not very large, three) chickens; when cold remove all the meat from the bones, also the skin, and chop or cut rather fine. Wash and separate two large heads of celery, if celery cannot be procured, a good substitute is the nice tender part of a cabbage, with celery seed added to flavor it. For dressing, see salad dressing.

LOBSTER SALAD.

Make a dressing of the yolks of four hard-boiled eggs, some salt, pepper, a little oil, mustard, and vinegar. Make these ingredients into a smooth paste about the consistency of cream. Mash the meat of the lobster with a little cold water, just enough to soften it, and cut up a head of lettuce into small pieces, and mix with it. Season the lettuce and meat with cayenne pepper, and a little salt, and mix them with the dressing just before sending to table. The different condiments must be in such proportion that no one shall predominate.

SWEET BREAD SALAD.
MRS. HERRON, CINCINNATI.

One dozen sweet breads, (first soak an hour in clear water,) boil, and pick to pieces, removing all gristle and fat; break up into quite small pieces. Pour over this the mayonnaise dressing, made of ten eggs. Lay on lettuce, and if your sweet breads are small mix with lettuce. This makes sufficient for forty guests, and is a delightful side dish.

POTATO SALAD.
MRS. J. QUETTING, BROOKLYN.

Boil a half dozen, or eight, good-sized potatoes in the skin, when done peel them, and cut in fine slices, cut a small piece of onion very fine. Take two hard boiled eggs, and rub the yolks in two tablespoonfuls of salad oil, add pepper, salt and vinegar, chop the whites of the eggs very fine, and add to the sauce. Pour the sauce over the potatoes, and mix well. There should be sauce enough just to moisten them thoroughly.

HAM SALAD.
MRS. NYE, CHILLICOTHE.

One pound of boiled ham, chopped fine, one-half dozen pickles, chopped fine. Make a dressing as you would for chicken salad, adding a little celery seed, but not as much salt.

CHICKEN SALAD DRESSING.
MRS. SILVEY.

Yolks of eight eggs, well beaten, one-quarter pound of sugar, (if preferred) one tablespoonful of salt, two of prepared mustard, a very little cayenne pepper, half cup cream, one pint of vinegar, one cup of butter; boil to the consistency of custard. Add some salad of oil if you prefer.

MAYONNAISE DRESSING.

MRS. HERRON.

Yolks of two hard boiled eggs, well mashed; add the yolks of two raw eggs, one teaspoonful dry mustard; salt and cayenne pepper to the taste. As much salad oil as you please, poured drop by drop, and well stirred in one tablespoonful of vinegar. This dressing is used for chicken salad dressing, and also for lettuce, tomatoes, salmon, sweet-breads and chopped celery.

PREPARED MUSTARD.

MRS. J. FULTON.

Two tablespoonfuls of mustard, one large teaspoonful of sugar, one-half teaspoonful of salt. Pour on enough boiling water to wet it. When cool add a tablespoonful of salad oil, and vinegar enough to make it thin.

MEATS, POULTRY, ETC.

TO CORN BEEF.

MRS. ALVAH BUCKINGHAM.

Have your beef or pork cut up in suitable pieces for cooking. Then pack them, not too tightly, in a tight hogshead or barrel, placing a weight on the top. Then make enough brine to cover it, in the following proportion: To four gallons of water use eight pounds of salt, two ounces of saltpetre, and one quart of molasses, place in a kettle, and bring it to a boil; skim thoroughly, then pour off in some vessel until it cools, then pour it over your beef. Your pieces for drying take out in six weeks and smoke. Let your corn beef, and pickled pork remain in the brine until wanted for use. If in the spring the brine moulds, pour it off and bring it to a boil again, skim as before, and pour it over the beef again hot.

VEAL PATÉ.

Three pounds of veal, chopped fine, before it is cooked. Five soda crackers rolled fine, piece of butter larger than an egg, one tablespoonful salt, one tablespoonful of pepper. Mix thoroughly together, mould into a loaf and put into a pan with a little water. Roast three hours, basting it often.

VEAL LOAF.
MRS. NYE, CHILLICOTHE.

Three pounds of clear veal, one quarter pound of salt pork, chopped fine, one tea-cup of cracker crumbs, one nutmeg, two eggs well beaten, two teaspoonfuls of pepper, two teaspoonfuls of salt, a little mace, parsley or sage, a little lemon peel and the juice of one lemon, a small piece of butter. Bake in pans, or steam it three hours, wrapped closely in a cloth.

VEAL CUTLET.

Pound your cutlets until tender, beat up the yolks of two or three eggs, with pepper and salt, grate a quantity of bread crumbs. First drop your cutlets into the egg, and then in the bread crumbs, and fry. A little parsley improves the flavor. You may use flour instead of bread crumbs if you prefer.

SAUSAGE MEAT.
MRS. NYE, CHILLICOTHE.

To one hundred pounds of chopped meat, add two and a half pounds of salt, ten ounces of black pepper, and eight ounces of well dried sage leaves. Mix well.

CHICKEN PUDDING.

MRS. C. PORTER.

Five eggs beaten very light, one pint of milk, one tablespoonful of butter, a little pepper and salt; put in flour sufficient to make a batter as thick as for pancakes; cut up a chicken, boil until tender, pick out the large bones, put it in a baking dish, pour over it the batter and bake until brown. You may add a few oysters if in season, and serve with the gravy the chicken was boiled in.

A Very Nice Way to Cook Chickens.

Cut the chicken up, put it in a pan and cover it with water; let it stew as usual, and when done make a thickening of cream, and flour, adding a piece of butter, pepper and salt. Have made and baked two short cakes, made as for pie crust, but rolled thin, and cut in small squares. This is much better than chicken pie, and more simple to make. Lay the crust on the dish, and pour the chicken and gravy over it while both are hot.

CHICKEN CROQUETTS.

MRS. HERRON, CINCINNATI.

Boil one large chicken, pick to pieces and chop fine; make a panada of three-quarters of a pound of light bread crumbs, a half pound of butter, and a little water; cook until the consistency of mush, and set away to cool. Add to the chicken, one nutmeg, pepper, and salt to taste, one teaspoonful chopped onion, one of parsley and a very little mace. Boil five eggs hard, rub the yolks and mix with the chicken, add the panada, mix well, and make out in shape of pears. Roll them in eggs beaten light, then in bread crumbs, and fry brown in hot lard, as you would fry doughnuts. You must have a pound of meat. Veal makes nice croquetts.

CHICKEN CROQUETTS. (No. 2.)

Take the white and dark meat of a nicely roasted or boiled chicken, (the former preferred as it contains the most nutriment,) chop it fine, and season highly with pepper and salt. Moisten it with a little of its own gravy, and form it into oval balls with the fingers, dip each one into an egg well beaten, and then roll in bread or cracker crumbs, and fry in boiling lard or butter. Serve on a hot platter, ornamenting the dish with slices of pickled beet, and sprig of parsley or celery leaves. A good way to shape croquetts is by using a wine or jelly glass.

OLD-FASHIONED POT-PIE.
MARTHA WELLS HALE.

Cut up one or two nice chickens, put into a deep pot, and boil until done. Then take some bread-dough, (a good time to make this is on baking day,) and after working in some shortening, just as if you were making ordinary light rolls. Make them out into rolls or dumplings, and set aside to rise. When the chicken is sufficiently done, make a rich gravy; about a half hour before you are ready to serve them, drop into the pot with your chicken and gravy your dumplings; cover tight, and do not lift the lid, *under any circumstances* until done. A half hour is sufficient to boil them. Serve immediately, for if allowed to stand they will fall.

BEEF, ALAMODE.

Procure a fine beefsteak, have it cut extra thick, then pound it well, season with salt and pepper; make a stuffing as you would for a turkey, spread it on the steak quite thick, then roll up and bind securely with tape, put it into a dripping-pan with water sufficient to cover it. Let it stew slowly for two or three hours, add boiling water if more water is needed. The gravy will require no thickening, but a glass of wine will improve it.

A Nice Breakfast Relish.

Chip some smoked beef, and drop into boiling water to soften. Let it lie ten minutes, and then put it into a skillet with a little boiling water, and stir gently for twenty minutes. Pour off the water, put in a little butter, and some pepper, and pour in a half tea-cup of cream five minutes before taking from the fire.

CHICKEN PIE.

MRS. NYE.

Line a pan with pastry, then fill with disjointed pieces of chicken, and strips or squares of dough; sprinkle with pepper and salt, sift in a very little flour, and add small pieces of butter; cover the top with pastry leaving a slit in the center; fill the pan with water, and let it bake an hour and a half. Just before serving fill the pan again with water. If the chicken is tough it should be boiled before putting in the pie, and the water used for the gravy.

BEEF BOUILLE.

Rub salt and pepper thoroughly into your beef, (the rump or brisket pieces are the best,) and steam it about five hours over water into which is put pepper, salt, sweet marjoram, summer savory, thyme, onions, carrots, two turnips cut fine, some parsley, celery and tomatoes if possible. When the meat is perfectly tender take it up; take out the carrots from the gravy, strain, thicken and boil. Pour over the meat just before placing it on the table.

ROLLED BEEFSTEAK.

AN OLD CINCINNATI HOUSEKEEPER.

Take a flank steak, wash and pound it well, chop one onion very fine and spread it over the steak, then sprinkle over it a teaspoonful of salt, a little red pepper, a teaspoonful of ground mace, a teaspoonful of ground allspice, a quarter of a teaspoonful of ground cloves and a half teaspoonful of nutmeg. Roll it up, and as you roll it sprinkle it with pepper, salt and a small quantity of spice, (the same you have been using,) tie firmly with a string; put it into a pot and just cover with water. Let it boil two hours, (keep it covered well with water,) until so soft that a fork will penetrate easily, then remove it from the pot, and set it where it will keep hot, and allow the gravy to stew down to a half pint. Thicken this with a small quantity of flour, add a small piece of butter, and pour this over the steak after it has been put on the dish for the table.

HASH.

Chop up your meat tolerably fine, also some cold boiled potatoes, season with a little butter, salt and pepper, add some water (very little), and let it cook well together; have it almost dry, then put it on a dish, form it nicely in an oval shape, smooth over the top, place it in the oven and bake a dark brown. Serve on this same dish. Cold corn beef makes very nice hash.

FRENCH HASH.

Chop up *very fine* any kind of cold meat, put it into a frying or stew pan, season with butter, salt and pepper, put in some water, and allow it to cook well; just before it is done put in a little cream. Have some bread nicely toasted, place it on a large dish, and put a spoonful of the hash on each piece, pouring any gravy that is in the dish over it. This makes a very nice breakfast dish.

VEGETABLES.

EGG PLANT.

Cut in slices half an inch thick, sprinkle with salt, and let them stand a few minutes to extract the bitter taste. Wash in cold water, wipe them dry; season with pepper, dip in yolk of egg, and then in flour or cracker crumbs, and fry in butter. If you wish them for breakfast, a good plan is to cut them the night before, sprinkle with salt, and soak in the morning in fresh water an hour before frying.

CORN OYSTERS. (No. 1.)

Take a dozen ears of corn, grate it off the cob, and add one pint of new milk, two teaspoonfuls of ground pepper, one teaspoonful of salt, one tea-cup of flour; stir together, and fry them small in hot butter.

CORN OYSTERS. (No. 2.)

Cut the corn through the grain, and use a knife to scrape the pulp from the cob. Make a batter of two eggs, well beaten, two tablespoonfuls of flour, a little salt and pepper, and about a half-pint of milk. Beat the whole well together, and drop a spoonful at a time into hot lard, and fry brown.

GREEN CORN PUDDING.

Cut the corn in the same way as for corn oysters. Take two eggs, one quart of milk, a little flour, some salt, and the corn, and beat all together well. It must be of a consistency to pour easily. Grease the dish well, (a common pudding dish,) and pour the mixture in, and bake with a quick heat for half an hour. Six ears of corn will be sufficient for a quart of milk.

SARATOGA POTATOES.

Slice the potatoes *very thin* on a cabbage cutter; lay them in cold water for an hour, or if you desire them for breakfast, let them stand in the water over night; then drain them, and spread on a dry towel; wipe each piece dry, and drop a few at a time in boiling lard as you would when frying crullers, brown lightly, and as they are done take out with a skimmer, lay on a plate, and sprinkle a little fine salt over them. A very nice dish for a lunch, is to have some of these potatoes piled up in pyramid form on a platter, and place mutton chops around them, with the large end down, and bone standing up to help support the cone of the pyramid. Of course this must be served hot.

CORN PUDDING.

MRS. STEWART, PA.

One quart of milk, two eggs, one-half cup of butter, one tablespoonful of sugar, one dozen ears of corn. Grate the corn from the cob, beat up the eggs, add the corn, and stir hard, then add the butter, sugar, and a little salt, and pepper, lastly the milk. Bake in a moderate oven about half an hour.

SALSIFY, OR OYSTER PLANT.

Scrape the roots, dropping them in cold water to prevent turning dark. Cut in pieces about an inch long, put them into a sauce-pan with hot water sufficient to cover, and let them stew until tender. Then turn off the water, mash them, and make a batter of two eggs, a little salt and butter, and flour sufficient for a thick batter; add this to the salsify, mix up, make in small cakes, and fry in hot lard. Serve on a hot water dish.

BOILED SALSIFY.

Wash and scrape nicely, cut in pieces about an inch in length, and boil until tender, but not broken. Then make a dressing of a cup of cream, or milk thickened with flour, a piece of butter, salt, and pepper, boil it, and then pour over the salsify. Serve hot.

SOUR BEANS.

MRS. QUETTING.

Cut in pieces, and boil string beans until they are done, drain through a sieve perfectly dry. Put into a sauce-pan a tablespoonful of butter, a teaspoonful of flour, pepper, salt, and a little vinegar, (about a tablespoonful,) put in the beans, and let all cook together five minutes. Just before taking up, beat an egg light, and add to it.

COLD SLAW.

Beat together the yolks of three eggs, add a tea-cup of cream, three tablespoonfuls best cider vinegar, a piece of butter size of an egg. Put all together on the fire, stirring constantly until it comes to a boil, and pour over the cabbage; which must be previously cut fine, with a little salt sprinkled through it, also a tablespoonful of horse-radish, or fine mixed mustard.

COLD SLAW. (Very Fine.)

Take a plate of cut cabbage, a teacupful of chopped celery, and a third of a tea-cup of grated horse-radish. Season with salt. Make a dressing as for lettuce, with the yolks of four eggs boiled hard, rubbed into a smooth paste, with oil, mustard, salt, pepper, and vinegar, stir this mixture into the cabbage a few moments before dinner.

SPINACH.

Pick it over and wash thoroughly, then boil in salt and water, pour over melted butter and vinegar, and sprinkle on some pepper, and serve either with poached eggs laid over the top, or with thinly sliced hard boiled eggs.

MACARONI.

Put the macaroni into a pot of boiling water, with a little salt in it, and let it cook ten minutes. Then pour on fresh hot water, and milk in equal quantities, and boil ten minutes more. Then put it into a deep dish, with alternate layers of butter, and grated cheese, until the dish is full, having macaroni on the top, with a little butter on it without cheese. Bake in an oven for half an hour.

STUFFED TOMATOES.

Scoop out the inside of a dozen large tomatoes, without spoiling their shape. Pass the inside through a sieve, and then mix it with grated bread-crumbs, salt, pepper, and any herbs you desire, or you may omit the herbs. Stew this about ten minutes, and then stuff the tomatoes with the mixture, tying a string round each to keep them in shape. Sprinkle them all over with fine bread-crumbs. Set them in a buttered dish, and bake them in an oven; before serving take off the strings. Egg plant may be cooked in the same manner.

TO STEW TOMATOES.

Wash, and pour boiling water over them; peel off the skins, and cut them up. Season with pepper, salt and butter, cook them in their own juice, half an hour. Thicken with bread-crumbs, and after ten minutes take them up.

ONIONS.

Boil in water until nearly done, and then pour over fresh hot water, with milk in it. Drain, and dress with drawn butter, and a little salt and pepper sprinkled over them.

BEETS.

They are usually plain· boiled, and dressed with melted butter, vinegar, pepper and salt.

NEW POTATOES.

Scrape the skins from them, and let them remain in cold water for an hour or two, then put them into your kettle, cover with water, and let them boil for a half hour; try them by sticking with fork. Then drain the water off; let stand a few minutes, make a sauce of a little milk thickened with flour, a piece of butter, salt, and pepper, pour over the potatoes, and serve hot.

MASHED POTATOES.

Prepare the potatoes nicely by paring, and washing, put them into a vessel, and cover with water; let them boil a half hour, or until they are tender; then drain the water from them, and let them steam with the lid partly off for ten minutes; then mash them perfectly smooth, and beat a good deal, dress them with salt, butter, and cream. Serve them hot. A very nice way to serve them is to press them through a colander with the potato masher in the dish you serve them in, but the dish must be *very hot*, also the potatoes, and it must be done quickly. They will be very light, and will have the appearance of macaroni in the dish.

GREEN PEAS.

Shell them, and drop into boiling water for half an hour. If not very young, a little soda, the size of a pea will improve the color, and make them tender. Dress them with butter, salt, and pepper.

CAULIFLOWER.

Take equal quantities of milk, and water, and when it boils, put in the cauliflowers, and boil until tender. Pour drawn butter over them, and send to table hot. Broccoli is cooked in the same way.

SQUASHES.

Cut them up, and remove the seeds, cook in hot water until tender. Then wash and dress with butter, salt and pepper. They are nice cut in thick slices, and fried as egg-plant.

WINTER SQUASH.

Cut the ends off, take out the seeds, cut in long strips, and set in the oven to bake until tender. Then send to the table in the skin in which they are baked. They are nearly equal to sweet potatoes.

PARSNIPS.

Scrape, and split them, and put into a pot of boiling water until tender. Dress with plenty of butter, salt and pepper. Or you may parboil them, mash, make into little cakes, dip them into beaten egg, and grated crackers, and fry in hot lard.

TURNIPS

Are boiled until tender, then mashed, and dressed like parsnips.

LETTUCE.

Make a dressing, either the mayonnaise or chicken salad dressing, put the mixture in the bottom of your salad bowl, and lay the lettuce, nicely arranged upon it. (It must be previously picked, and washed well.) When you serve at table, cut up the salad, and mix with a spoon, and fork the dressing before helping it.

BOILED HOMINY.

Wash it well, and put it in your vessel on the stove, in sufficient cold water to cover it; it must boil constantly for three or four hours, and as the water boils away, have your tea-kettle on the stove boiling, and fill up from it. It will be dark if you allow it to stop boiling, or if you do not always fill up with boiling water. Season with butter, salt, and cream.

FRIED HOMINY.

Take cold boiled hominy, mash it up as well as you can, beat up one or two eggs, (according to the quantity of hominy you have,) stir them in, also a little flour, salt, and a very little butter, make into cakes, and fry in hot lard. This is a very nice dish for breakfast.

SMALL HOMINY, OR SAMP.

Put it on in boiling water, and let boil until it is thick, stirring frequently, just before taking up put in some salt. This is a very nice breakfast dish, eaten either with sugar and cream, or butter and cream as you prefer. If any is left over set it away, and fry the next morning as you would corn meal mush.

TO BOIL RICE.

Pick and wash a teacupful of rice, and put it in a rice kettle, with a pint of cold water; cover close, and let it boil until done. Let it steam a few minutes after it is tender, so that every grain will stand alone. It will cook in twenty minutes over a bright fire.

FRIED APPLES.

Take apples that are not very sour, wash, quarter and core them, (but do not peel,) put them into a frying-pan with a piece of butter size of an egg, and about one tea-cup of sugar. Cover them with a plate, and let them fry slowly, stirring occasionally until done.

MACARONI, WITHOUT CHEESE.
MRS. J. FULTON.

Put it on in a little water. Let it come to a hard boil, then drain off the water. Put it on again with milk, and a large lump of butter. Boil until quite tender, and while hot mix in a little cream, and add some sugar, nutmeg or cinnamon, or you may omit them.

SAVORY CABBAGE.

MRS. J. FULTON.

Cook them until they are about half done in water; then pour that water off, and put them in again with about half milk and water until done. Cooked in this way they are almost as nice as cauliflower. Dress them as you would cauliflower. Any strong vegetable like turnips, cabbage, etc., are better for changing the water when half done.

A GOOD WAY TO COOK ONIONS.

Boil them first in milk and water; this diminishes the strong taste, then chop them up and put them into a stew-pan with a little milk, butter, salt and pepper, and let them stew about fifteen minutes. This gives them a fine flavor, and they can be served up very hot.

Any vegetable is improved by being boiled in water to which a little salt has been added, it makes them much more tender.

Onions are probably more improved by being cooked in salt water than any other vegetable. Much of their unpleasant smell is taken away, and a peculiar sweetness, and improved aroma is decidedly apparent.

PICKLES AND CATSUP.

ROUGH AND READY PICKLES.

MRS. HERRON, CINCINNATI.

Slice six dozen cucumbers, and one-half peck green tomatoes, one dozen green bull-nose peppers, one ounce white silver onions. Salt separately, let stand over night. Next morning press perfectly dry, and mix all together, having chopped the onions and peppers fine, put in one-half tea-cup ground black pepper, one-half cup allspice, one-half pound white mustard seed, one ounce celery seed, horse-radish and a few cloves. Cover well with good vinegar, and let come to a boil. For every gallon of mixture add a half pound brown sugar.

PICKLES. (No. 1.)

An excellent way to put up pickles that will keep a year or more: Drop them into boiling hot water, but not boil them; let them remain ten minutes, wipe them dry, and drop into cold, spiced vinegar, and they will not need to be put into salt and water. The above is a rule which has been thoroughly tested, and has found to be a most excellent one.

PICKLES. (No. 2.)

MRS. H. STURGES.

To one hundred cucumbers, one pint of salt. Pour boiling water on them, and let them stand twenty-four hours, wash in hot water. Put them in jars with spices and pour over them boiling vinegar.

PICKLES. (No. 3.)

Lay cucumbers in salt one week. Then put them in cold water until they are the proper freshness, (taste them.) Pour boiling vinegar over them; putting in the vinegar, cinnamon or cloves, and a small piece of alum.

RED CABBAGE AND CAULIFLOWER.

Slice into a colander your cabbage and cauliflower, sprinkle each layer with salt, let it drain two days, then put it into a jar with boiling vinegar, enough to cover it, or a few slices of beet-root may be added. Select the purple red cabbage. Those who like spices will boil pepper, corn, mustard seed, and any other whole spices with the vinegar. Cauliflower cut in branches and thrown in after being salted will be a beautiful red.

TOMATO PICKLE.
MRS. WILLS.

One peck green tomatoes sliced, one dozen onions sliced, sprinkle with salt, and let them stand until the following day, then drain them well. One box mustard (prepared), one and a half ounces black pepper (whole), one ounce cloves, one ounce yellow mustard seed, one ounce allspice. Put in a kettle layers of tomatoes, onions and spices until it is all in, then cover completely with vinegar. Let the whole boil (after it commences to boil) twenty minutes or a half hour. This is a *splendid pickle*.

CUCUMBER PICKLES. (Extra Nice.)
MRS. HERRON, CINCINNATI.

Make a strong brine of salt and water, put your cucumbers into it fresh, let them remain in it for nine days, pouring it off, and scalding it every second day, pouring it on the cucumbers boiling. When this is done take some vinegar, (if it is very strong two-thirds vinegar, and one-third water,) heat it boiling hot, pour over your pickles, having first covered them with cabbage or vine leaves, and let them stand twenty-four hours. Then take cider vinegar *of the first quality*, sweeten with brown sugar to taste; say one and a half pounds to two gallons of vinegar. Have ready allspice, sticks of cinnamon, black pepper, (*whole*,) mustard seed, caraway seed, celery seed, and race ginger. Put these all into the vinegar while heating. Pour off the vinegar which you put on first, and pour on this last preparation. Tie up securely so as to exclude the air.

This same process is used for mangoes; by no means omit the caraway seed and celery seed, also add horse-radish in slices. I often use cucumbers for making mangoes; take the inside out with a knife, and stuff as you would mangoes, and tie up.

STUFFING FOR CUCUMBER MANGOES.
MRS. HERRON, CINCINNATI.

Wash a pound of white race ginger very clean, pour boiling water on it, and let stand twenty-four hours; slice it thin, and dry it, one pound of horse-radish dried and scraped, one pound mustard-seed, one pound chopped onion, one ounce mace, one nutmeg pounded fine, two ounces of tumeric, and a handful of whole black pepper. Make these ingredients into a paste with a quarter pound of mustard, and a large cup of olive oil, put a clove of garlic into each mango. This is sufficient stuffing for forty cucumbers.

TOMATO CATSUP.

MRS. DYE.

To one gallon of strained tomato pulp, take four tablespoonfuls of salt, four of black pepper, two of allspice, two pods of red peppers. Boil all together until it is quite thick; add a very small quantity of vinegar and sugar. One onion to a gallon of juice is an improvement. Put the ground spice in muslin bags, or it will make the catsup very dark.

TOMATO CATSUP. (Splendid.)

MRS. WALTER DUN.

Boil one bushel tomatoes until tender, rub them through a colander, add two quarts cider vinegar, one and a quarter pounds salt, one quarter pound black pepper, two ounces cayenne pepper, three grated nutmegs, one quarter pound allspice, six onions, three pounds brown sugar. Boil down, and when cold strain through a sieve to remove the onion, then bottle. This receipt I use constantly, and thick it cannot be excelled.

TOMATO SAUCE.

MRS. STANTON.

To make one gallon, take one gallon of green tomatoes, one dozen large onions, one dozen green peppers (seeds taken out), all kinds of spices to suit the taste, one large cup of ground mustard, one cup half full of good olive oil, two tablespoonfuls of salt (more if your taste requires). Cover the whole with strong vinegar, and boil about one hour. Put away in small jars, paste paper over them to exclude the air.

CHOW-CHOW.

Chop fine two quarts of green tomatoes, two quarts of white onions, one dozen green peppers, one dozen green cucumbers, one large head of cabbage. Season with mustard and celery seeds to suit the taste. Cover with the best cider vinegar. Boil two hours slowly, stiring continually. As soon as you take it from the stove, add two tablespoonfuls of salad oil. Cover tight and keep in a cool place.

MIXED PICKLE.

MRS. HERRON, CINCINNATI.

One head cabbage, two dozen large sized cucumbers, one dozen good sized green tomatoes, one-half dozen white onions, three green peppers. Slice the onions, pour boiling water on them, and let them stand fifteen minutes, chop the other ingredients, and mix all together; sprinkle with salt in layers, and let stand one hour, drain and cover with vinegar for twenty-four hours. Then take fresh vinegar, and to every gallon of pickle, after draining, put two ounces of cloves, two ounces of mustard seed, black pepper, mace, celery seed and horse-radish as much as you think fit. Boil all together fifteen or twenty minutes, and bottle tight.

CHILI SAUCE.

MRS. HERRON.

Two dozen silver onions, four small red peppers, twelve ripe tomatoes, peeled, chopped fine, and put together with two tablespoonfuls of brown sugar, two and a half quarts of cider vinegar, or one and a half wine vinegar, and one quart of water. Salt to taste. Stew gently for four or five hours, until all is soft, and beginning to thicken. Seal hot.

SPICED PEACHES AND PLUMS.

MISS JENNY HERRON.

One peck of peaches pared, three pints of vinegar, three and a half pounds of sugar, three nutmegs grated or broken up, one ounce cloves, one ounce cinnamon. Pare the peaches, place them in a jar, and stew the spice through them, or tie up in bags. Boil the sugar and vinegar together a few minutes, and pour hot over the peaches. Repeat this process for three consecutive days, the fourth day put the peaches in, and boil all together for ten minutes. Use the same rule for plums, but do not take quite so much vinegar.

PEACH MANGOES.

MISS JENNY HERRON.

One peck of peaches two-thirds ripe, throw into strong salt, and water for twelve hours. Wipe dry, cut in half, take out the stone, and make the filling as follows: One-quarter pound white mustard-seed, one-quarter pound black-mustard seed, one pound brown sugar, two tablespoonfuls of tumeric, one tablespoonful cloves (ground), four tablespoonfuls sweet oil, one tablespoonful celery-seed, two onions chopped fine, two red peppers chopped fine. This makes enough for two dozen more peaches than the above. Sew up, and leave in vinegar containing one pound brown sugar to the gallon, three or four red peppers, a little scraped horse-radish, and some bruised ginger-root.

SPICED GOOSEBERRIES.

To two gallons of fruit add nine pounds of sugar. Boil together until soft, and add one pint of good vinegar, allspice, cloves and cinnamon to your taste.

CHOW-CHOW.

MRS. E. H. BUCKINGHAM.

One-half bushels of green tomatoes, one dozen onions, one dozen green peppers chopped fine; sprinkle over the mass a pint of salt, let it stand over night, then drain off the brine; cover it with good vinegar, let it cook one hour slowly, then drain and pack in a jar; take two pounds of sugar, two tablespoonfuls of cinnamon, same of allspice, one each of cloves and pepper, one-half cup of ground mustard, one pint of horse-radish, and vinegar enough to mix thin.

When boiling hot pour over the pickle packed in the jar, and cover tight. Then it is ready for use, and will keep for months.

ONION PICKLES.

Peel one-half gallon silver onions, put into strong brine for three days; take out and simmer in milk and water for a short time, then take out and dry; put them in a jar, and pour hot vinegar over them flavored with mace.

MANGOES.
MRS. NYE, CHILLICOTHE.

Put melons in brine for two weeks, then soak in clear water over night, simmer one day in vinegar, slit, take the seeds out, and fill with the following: Cut cabbage fine, and salt over night, squeeze out the water, and add one pint of grated horse-radish, one-half pint of mustard seed, (brown and white,) three cloves of garlic, one pound of brown sugar, one-quarter of a pint of olive oil, cloves, mace, ginger and allspice, (use the best cider vinegar). Put one small pepper in each melon, when filled sew them up, pour boiling vinegar (with a little sugar in it) over them, and tie up tight. Best when one year old.

WHITE WALNUTS.

Take them when so soft a pin will run through easily. Boil salt and water strong enough to bear an egg, skim it, and when cold pour over the walnuts. Let them stand in this brine fourteen days, and then throw them into cold water for two days. Boil them in weak vinegar, and let them lie in this a week. Simmer enough strong vinegar to cover them. Mix together grated horse-radish, cloves, mustard-seed, and red pepper. Put the walnuts into the jar in alternate layers with the condiments, and pour the scalding vinegar over them.

EAST INDIA PICKLE.
MRS. J. QUETTING, BROOKLYN.

One-half peck of green tomatoes, one-half peck of sliced ripe tomatoes, two heads of cauliflower, one peck of small cucumbers;

salt this and let it stand twenty-four hours, then drain and freshen a little, add a handful of scraped horse-radish, three heads of celery, one-half ounce of turmeric, one-half ounce of cloves, one-eighth of a pound of ground pepper, one-half pound of white mustard-seed, one-half pound of flour of mustard, one-eighth of a pound of sugar, one-half ounce of cinnamon; put in a kettle with cold vinegar, let it boil fifteen minutes, (watch carefully as it burns easily,) pour it on hot. Mix the turmeric, one-half a tea-cup of flour and mustard together in a paste with cold vinegar, and stir in when boiling, to thicken.

WATERMELON SWEET PICKLES.

Two pounds of watermelon, or muskmelon rinds, boiled in pure water until tender. Drain them well. Then make a syrup of two pounds of sugar, one quart of vinegar, half an ounce of mace, an ounce of cinnamon, and some roots of ginger, boiled until thick, and pour over the melons boiling hot. Drain off the syrup, heat it until boiling hot, and pour over the melons three days in succession. They are very nice, and will keep two years.

HIGDON PICKLE.

MRS. C. PORTER.

One gallon of vinegar, one pound sugar, one head of cabbage, one-half pint of horse-radish cut fine, one-half dozen large onions, eight spoonfuls of yellow mustard-seed, four spoonfuls of brown mustard-seed, six ounces of ground black pepper, three ounces of ground mustard, three ounces of ginger, cinnamon, mace, race ginger, and cloves enough when pulverized to make four spoonfuls, celery seed to taste, one pint green radish pods, one-half pint radish seeds, as many green tomatoes as the vinegar will cover; the tomatoes must be sliced, salted and squeezed dry. The sugar and vinegar must be boiled, the onions sliced, and all put into a kettle with the boiling vinegar until well heated. Keep in a stone jar covered tight.

BREAD AND BISCUITS.

YEAST. (Very Fine.)

Boil five or six pared potatoes; when soft, mash them in the boiling water over the fire. Put in a half teacupful of dried hops, and let them boil ten minutes (not longer,) and then strain through a colander. Put in a pinch of salt, and stir well; thin it with milk-warm water until the consistency of thin waffle batter. When luke-warm stir in a teacupful of liquid yeast. Set it near the back part of the stove, or in a tolerably warm place to rise, and in twelve or fourteen hours it will be light. If not, put in a little more yeast. If the weather is warm it will not require to be placed near the stove. If you wish dry yeast, rub in sifted corn meal until it is a dry dough, and spread thin on dishes or waiters to dry in the air, but not in the sun.

YEAST. (Splendid.)
MRS. E. E. FILLMORE.

Boil in one gallon of water a small handful of hops, and three or four potatoes. Put into a jar flour sufficient to make a thin batter, with one cup of sugar, one cup of ginger, one cup of salt; on this pour through a colander the boiling yeast water and potatoes. When sufficiently cool, add yeast to raise, and jug for use.

FRENCH ROLLS.
MRS. HOGE.

Take your dough, (judge of the quantity by size of your family,) work in a heaping tablespoonful of lard or butter, and let stand in a tolerably cool place for four hours, then knead again, and let alone for three hours more, make into rolls by rolling out very lightly pieces of the dough into round cakes, and folding over not quite in the center, then let them rise the third time one hour, bake a half hour or less if the oven is hot.

RAISED BISCUIT.

MRS. HOGE.

One quart of milk, three-quarters cup of lard, or butter, (half and half will do,) three-quarters of a cup of yeast, two of sugar, (if liked,) one teaspoonful of salt, flour sufficient for a soft dough. Mix over night, warm the milk, and melt the lard, or butter in it. In the morning roll out into a sheet three-quarters of an inch thick, and cut into round cakes, let them rise twenty minutes, and bake about twenty minutes.

BISCUIT.

Three pints of flour, three teaspoonfuls of salt, three teaspoonfuls of baking powder, one large spoonful of lard, one pint of sweet milk. If you wish to use sour milk use soda instead of baking powder. Handle as little as possible, roll thin, cut with a cutter, and bake.

MARYLAND BISCUIT.

One quart of sifted flour, one tablespoonful of lard. Mix to a stiff dough with cold water, beat half an hour, and make out in small cakes, with the fingers press flat, and bake in a quick oven. Add a little salt to the flour.

MARYLAND BISCUIT.

MRS. NYE, CHILLICOTHE.

Three pints of flour, three teaspoonfuls of salt, six ounces of lard, rubbed through the flour, two-thirds of a pint of cold water. Knead or pound until the dough blisters, mould into small biscuits with the hand, and bake immediately.

CREAM BISCUIT.

One pint of sour cream, to which add, one teaspoonful of soda dissolved in a little warm water, a pinch of salt, add flour sufficient to roll and cut.

SPONGE BISCUIT.

One quart of milk warmed, with four teaspoonfuls of lard. When warm add two teaspoonfuls of salt, one tea-cup of yeast and enough flour to make a stiff batter. When very light, drop in spoonfuls on a sheet iron pan, and bake in a quick oven.

BREAD.
MRS. NYE.

Six potatoes boiled quickly, and mashed fine, one pint of flour, mixed with them, and three pints of potato water. When about lukewarm add one quart of yeast. Cover closely and set to rise. When light enough add seven quarts of flour, and knead well. Cover closely to exclude the air, let it rise until it cracks, work into loaves, put them into the pans to rise again, and then bake three-quarters of an hour. This makes eight loaves.

PARKER HOUSE ROLLS.
MRS. NYE, CHILLICOTHE.

Take two quarts of wheat flour, make a hole in the center, put in a piece of butter size of an egg, a little salt, one tablespoonful of white sugar; pour over this a pint of milk previously boiled, and allowed to cool, and one-half a tea-cup of yeast. When the sponge is light mould fifteen minutes and let it rise again; then cut into round cakes; when light flatten with the rolling pin, put a small piece of butter on each, and fold them in the middle. Put in pans to rise, and bake in a quick oven.

PUFFS, OR POP-OVERS.
MRS. NYE.

One pint sour cream, one pint of flour, three or four eggs beaten separately, one tea-spoon of soda (not full) mixed in the flour, and a little salt. Bake in muffin tins. Nice for tea.

POCKET ROLLS.
MRS. NYE.

To one pint of sponge, add one quarter of a pint each of butter and lard, three tablespoonfuls of sugar, seven pints of flour, knead well. Let it rise, then roll out, cut with a biscuit cutter, dip each piece in melted butter, double it over, and place in the pans to rise. Let them rise two hours before you wish them baked. Should the dough rise too rapidly work it down to prevent its falling. This may be done several times.

INDIAN MEAL ROLLS.
MISS BARROWS.

One large cup of flower, two large cups of meal, from a tablespoon to a half cup of sugar. according to taste, a pinch of salt, two eggs, one pint of sour milk, and one teaspoonful of soda dissolved in a half cup of hot or cold water. If you do not use sour milk, wet it up with water using soda and cream of tartar, as you would make up sweet milk muffins.

BROWN FLOUR ROLLS.
MISS BARROWS.

Same as the above, only using brown flour instead of meal.

SODA BISCUIT. (No. 1.)

One quart of flour, two teaspoonfuls of cream of tarter, and one of soda, one tablespoonful of shortening ; mix up with sour milk, put the cream of tarter, and soda in the flour, and run through the sieve twice.

SODA BISCUIT. (No. 2.)

Sift two teaspoonfuls of cream of tarter in with one quart of flour, rub in a piece of butter size of an egg. Dissolve one teaspoonful of soda in two-thirds of a pint of sweet milk or warm water, and mix into the flour quickly. Knead the dough only what is necessary to bring it together, and get it ready for the oven as quickly as possible, and bake immediately.

INDIAN CORN BISCUIT.

One quart of corn meal, one pint of wheat flour, sifted together, and stirred into three pints of milk; add a teaspoonful of salt. Beat four eggs, the yolks and whites separately. First stir the yolks into the batter; then add the whites, and a small teaspoonful of soda the last thing. Have ready buttered some small pans, nearly fill them with the batter, and set into the hot oven immediately. Bake quickly, and turn from the pans as soon as done, and serve at once. They should puff up so as to more than fill the pans.

RUSK.
MRS. M. A. HOGE.

One pint of warm milk, one-half cup of butter, one of sugar, two eggs, one teaspoonful of salt, two tablespoonfuls of yeast. Make a sponge with the milk, yeast and flour for a thin batter. In the morning add the butter, sugar and eggs beaten well together; add flour sufficient to make a soft dough. Mould into rolls, and let rise until very light.

BREAD CAKES.

Take dry bread, pour over it boiling water, and cover for a few minutes, then mash fine. Add one pint of butter-milk, a small teaspoonful of saleratus, four eggs, beaten separately, a little salt, and flour enough to bake well. Bake on a griddle.

MUFFINS. (No. 1.)

One pint of flour, two well beaten eggs, one teaspoonful of butter, two tablespoonfuls of yeast, and what sweet milk it will take to make them a little thicker than griddle cakes. Mix them over night, and bake them on buttered griddle in muffin rings.

MUFFINS. (No. 2.)

Take one pint of milk, four eggs (beaten light), a tea-cup of home-made yeast, a few grated bread-crumbs, and one quart of flour. Beat them into a smooth batter, and let them stand three, or four hours to rise. Bake them in rings, which must be well buttered.

RICE AND FLOUR MUFFINS.

Half a tea-cup of flour, one tea-cup of boiled rice, one pint and a half of milk, and three eggs (beaten separately.) The batter must be as thin as for griddle cakes. Bake with a quick heat in muffin rings or gem pans.

CORN MUFFINS.

MRS. STURGES.

Three cups corn meal, one-half cup wheat flour, three eggs, beaten separately, two spoonfuls of butter, one teaspoonful of soda, a little salt, and one pint sweet milk.

SALLY LUNN.

One quart of flour, four eggs, one-half cup of butter melted in one cup of milk, one cup warm water, four tablespoonfuls yeast, one teaspoonful of salt, one-half teaspoonful of soda dissolved in hot water. Beat the eggs light (separately) add the milk, water, butter, soda and salt. Stir in the flour and yeast, beat well. Set to rise in buttered pans, let stand six hours, and bake three-quarters of an hour in a moderate oven.

SALLY LUNN. (Very Fine.)

Three eggs beaten separately very light, one pint of milk warmed, half a tea-cup of butter melted, half a tea-cup of yeast, two pints of flour, and a teaspoonful and a half of salt. Beat well and pour into a buttered pan in which it is to be baked, and when light bake with a quick heat. You can add to this a tea-cup of sugar if desired.

WAFFLES. Very Fine.

One pint sweet milk, half a tea-cup of butter-milk or clabber, two eggs (beaten separately), one pint and a half of flour, and a piece of lard size of a small egg melted, and put in the batter. Beat well for fifteen minutes. Grease the waffle irons, fill them with the batter, and bake quickly, turning the irons so that both sides will be browned. If you have no sweet milk it will do to make them entirely of sour or buttermilk.

RICE WAFFLES.

One and a half tea-cups of boiled rice, warm it with a pint of milk. Mix it smooth, then take it from the fire, stir in a pint of cold milk, and a teaspoonful of salt, beat four eggs very light, and stir in with flour for a stiff batter.

DROP CAKES.

One coffee-cup of corn meal scalded with either milk or water, add a little salt, and one egg beaten light. Drop into hot lard, and fry until done. These are very nice for breakfast. I often make them in this way, and drop on the griddle.

CORN MEAL BATTER CAKES.

Pour boiling milk over sifted corn meal and beat until lukewarm. Then add a little salt, two tablespoonfuls of flour, and three eggs well beaten. Bake on a griddle. The milk and meal must be in such proportion as will make a thin batter; say a pint of meal to a quart of boiled milk.

CORN BREAD.

One pint of milk, two eggs beaten light, a tablespoonful of melted butter, a little salt, one teaspoonful of cream of tarter, one-half teaspoonful of soda, enough meal to make a thin batter.

Or, four eggs beaten separately, four tablespoonfuls of sugar, one pint of milk, two coffee-cups of Indian meal, one teaspoonful of soda, two of cream of tarter, small piece of butter, and one cup of cream.

CORN CAKES.

One pint cold mush, one-half tea-cup of flour, rubbed well into the mush, with one tablespoonful of lard, from one to three eggs. If the mush is too stiff use water to thin it. Bake rapidly on a griddle.

CREAM CAKES.

One quart of sour cream, four eggs, one teaspoonful of saleratus, one teaspoonful of salt, flour sufficient for a stiff batter. Bake in muffin rings.

FLANNEL CAKES.

One coffee-cup of sour milk, two eggs beaten separately, and very light, flour sufficient to make a good batter; just before baking add one teaspoonful of soda dissolved in a little water, also a little salt, add the whites of the eggs last. Bake on a hot griddle.

BROWN FLOUR MUSH.

Put two pints of boiling water in a kettle on the stove. Mix up a little of the brown meal in cold water as thick as you would to make starch; then pour it into the boiling water, stir in dry meal until you have it about as thick as for ordinary mush. Then thin it again with boiling water, until about the consistency of starch, or as it was at the start, just let it come to a boil again, and pour into moulds, and eat as you would cracked wheat.

GEMS.

Into cold water stir Graham flour sufficient to make a batter a trifle thicker than that used for ordinary griddle cakes. Bake from one-half to three-quarters of an hour in a hot oven in small tin patty-pans two inches square and three-fourths of an inch deep.

DIAMONDS.

Pour boiling water on Graham flour, stirring rapidly until all the flour is wet. Too much stirring makes it tough. It should be about as thick as can be stirred easily with a strong iron spoon. Place the dough with plenty of flour upon a moulding board, and knead it for two or three minutes. Roll out one-half an inch thick and cut in small cakes or rolls. If a large quantity is required, roll about three-fourths of an inch and cut with a knife in diamond shape. Bake in a very hot oven forty-five minutes.

GRAHAM BISCUIT.

Make some Graham mush (as above). When cool mix with it Graham flour sufficient to roll well. Knead for a few minutes, roll three-fourths of an inch thick, cut with a common biscuit cutter, and bake in a hot oven from thirty to forty-five minutes.

BROWN BREAD.

Take two and a half pounds of Graham flour, add one pound of brown sugar, a little salt, half tea-cup of home-made yeast, and one quart of warm water. Mix them all together with a pudding stick. Let it rise like wheat bread; but it must not be kneaded. Grease the tins, and bake in a moderate oven.

BOSTON BROWN BREAD.
MRS. E. BUCKINGHAM.

Two cups of corn meal, two cups of Graham flour, one cup of wheat flour, one teaspoonful of soda, two-thirds of a cup of molasses, one and a half pints of sweet milk, beat well and pour into a tin mould with a close lid; boil in a kettle of water from three to four hours, be sure that the water boils all the time, and keep it filled up as high as the bread is in the vessel. Always fill up with boiling water. When sufficiently done take out of the mould, and set in a hot oven for ten minutes.

GRAHAM CUP CAKES.

One and a half pints of Graham flour, one-half pint of wheat flour, four eggs, one-half pint of milk, one-quarter of a teaspoonful of soda, one teaspoonful of salt, one of sugar. Bake three-quarters of an hour.

ANOTHER OF SAME.
MISS BARROWS.

One cup of milk to one cup of Graham flour, a little salt; beat a great deal until very light. Bake in gem cups.

PIES, PUDDINGS AND DESSERTS.

PUFF PASTE.

MRS. E. BUCKINGHAM.

One pound of flour, break into it one egg, add a piece of butter size of an egg, and a teaspoonful of salt. Mix with cold water, and work until it is a smooth paste. Divide one pound of butter into six parts, roll the paste one-half inch thick, and spread one part of butter on, fold up, roll out again, spread on another part, and so on until the six parts are all used. Some persons use lard instead of butter; it makes very nice paste, but not quite as light, or so finely flavored as butter.

LEMON PIE.

MRS. M. A. HOGE.

Three eggs, three cups of sugar, two lemons, three tablespoonfuls of corn starch. Place on the stove a pint and a half of water, when it boils, stir the starch into it, then a piece of butter size of an egg. Beat the yolks and sugar well together, and when the starch water is cool, stir in the sugar and egg, then squeeze the juice of the lemon, and grate the peel in (not quite all,) and lastly add the whites beaten light. This is a delicious lemon pie—sufficient to make three.

LEMON PIE. (No. 2.)

MRS. HERRON.

One tea-cup of cold water, two tablespoonfuls flour, mixed smooth in water, two tea-cups of sugar, three eggs beaten separately, the whites added just as the mixture goes into the oven, juice and rind of one lemon. This will make two pies.

MINCE MEAT. (Extra.)

MRS. GRANT, PHILADELPHIA.

Five pounds of beef, two and a half of suet, five pounds of raisins, three pounds of currants, six pounds of chopped apples, one pound of citron, two and a half of sugar, four lemons, (juice and rind,) four oranges, one pint rose water, three nutmegs, two tablespoonfuls of ground cinnamon, one teaspoonful of cloves, one pint of wine, one pint of brandy. Add stewed apples and cider before baking.

MINCE MEAT.

Boil four pounds of beef and chop fine. Pick and chop three pounds of suet, wash two pounds of currants, and stone one pound of raisins, grate the peel of two lemons, and add the juice, an ounce of sliced citron, and twelve large apples chopped fine. Mix these ingredients with three pounds of sugar, half a pint of wine, and the same of brandy or cider, add nutmeg and mace to your taste. Bake this in puff paste with a lid on top.

APPLE CUSTARD PIE.

Take about one quart of stewed apples, one-half pound of sugar, small piece of butter; run through the colander. Then add the yolks of six eggs (well beaten), a little cinnamon and nutmeg.

POTATO PIE.

Boil one pound of potatoes, peel them, mash them through a colander. Stir to a cream three-quarters of a pound of sugar, and three-quarters of a pound of butter, add to this gradually a glass of wine, and one of brandy, a teaspoonful of powdered mace and cinnamon, one grated nutmeg, the juice and grated peel of one large lemon. Then beat six eggs very light, and add them by degrees to the mixture alternately with the potato.

PUMPKIN PIE.

MRS. NYE, CHILLICOTHE.

One quart of stewed and strained pumpkin, one teaspoonful of salt, one-quarter of a pound of butter, one pint of sugar, yolks of four eggs, one gill of rose water, one-half grated nutmeg, three tablespoonfuls of cinnamon, and one pint of milk. Lastly add the whites of the eggs well beaten. Line your pans with a nice crust, and fill with the above, using no top crust. Potato pie may be made as above, substituting potatoes (either sweet or Irish) instead of the pumpkin.

COCOANUT PIE.

MRS. NYE, CHILLICOTHE.

Soak two cups of dessicated cocoanut in one pint of milk, beat together the yolks of four eggs, and one-half cup of sugar, butter the size of an egg, and half grated nutmeg. Mix all well together and put it in to your crust, use no top crust, but beat the whites of the eggs with some sugar, and spread over the top.

COCOANUT PIE.

MRS. HERRON.

The weight of one cocoanut in sugar, one-half the weight in butter, five eggs, the milk of the nut and one pint of milk, grated peel and juice of one lemon. Beat the eggs and sugar together, add the milk, and melt the butter and put in. This will make four pies.

MARLBOROUGH PIE OR PUDDING.

MRS. ADAMS.

One quart of apples after cooking, run through the colander. Take twelve eggs beat separately very light, one-quarter of a pound of butter, six spoonfuls of sugar, one nutmeg, one lemon, grate the rind and add the juice.

DAUPHINES.

Line a pudding-dish with puff-paste, and put into it a thin layer of sweetmeats or stewed apples. Boil a custard of a pint of milk, three eggs, two tablespoonfuls of sugar, and one of flour until it thickens; flavor with vanilla, and pour over the fruit. Bake in a moderate oven, and when it is cold make an icing of whites of eggs and sugar, and pour over the top, set it in a moderately heated oven to dry.

INDIAN PUDDING.

MRS. H. STURGES.

Boil one quart of milk, remove it from the fire and stir in one cup of corn meal, and one of molasses; then put it on the fire again, and stir until it boils; add four eggs well beaten, butter the size of an egg, a half cup of cold milk, a little salt and ginger, put into a pudding-dish, and bake two hours.

ENGLISH PUDDING.

MRS. H. STURGES.

One pound brown sugar, one-half pound of butter, one pound of bread-crumbs, one pound of stoned raisins, one-half pound of currants, one-quarter of a pound of citron, eight eggs, two nutmegs. Boil six hours or longer. Can keep as you would fruit cake.

LEMON PUDDING.

MISS BRADLEY.

Ten eggs (beaten separately very light), one cup of sugar, one lemon. Stir the yolks of the eggs and sugar together very light, then grate half of the rind of the lemon, and also the pulp in with the sugar and eggs, then beat the whites of the eggs light, and put in the other half of the lemon (grated), and mix all together, beating very thoroughly. Bake in a pudding-dish about a half hour.

QUEEN OF PUDDINGS.

MRS. FENNER.

One pint of bread-crumbs, one quart of milk, one cup of sugar, yolks of four eggs, (well beaten,) butter size of an egg, grated rind of one lemon, mix all well together. Put in a pudding-dish, and bake until done, but not watery. Whip the whites of the eggs, and then beat into them one cup of sugar, in which stir the juice of the lemon; after the pudding has cooled some, spread over the top a layer of jelly or preserves of any kind. Pour the whites of the eggs on this, and replace in the oven, and bake lightly. Eat with cream.

COTTAGE PUDDING.

One tea-cup of white sugar, four tablespoonfuls melted butter, one teaspoonful of soda, one cup of sweet milk, one pint sifted flour, two teaspoonfuls of cream of tarter, and one egg. Beat the sugar, and butter to a cream, then add the egg well beaten, then the milk with the soda in it, lastly the flour with the cream of tarter in it. Bake in a cake-pan, one hour and a half.

Sauce for the above.—Two tea-cups of sugar, one tea-cup of butter, one dessertspoon of flour, mixed with a little water, one tea-cup of wine added last.

BROWN BETTY PUDDING.

Pare and slice a number of apples, butter a dish, and put in a layer of apples, and then a layer of bread-crumbs, with sugar, and butter, nutmeg, and cinnamon, alternate them until the dish is full. If the apples are not tart add lemon juice; put into the dish a tea-cup of water, and bake in a moderate oven until brown (an hour is generally sufficient). Serve in the same dish, or turn out on a platter, and eat either warm or cold with sauce or cream.

BREAD PUDDING.

Take a baker's loaf of bread and cut it in slices, spread each slice with butter, put it in a pan, and pour a quart of boiling milk over it, let it stand over night. In the morning beat seven eggs (very light), one-quarter pound sugar, one or two pounds of raisins, and spices to the taste, cinnamon, nutmeg and mace. Bake as you would pound cake and eat with sauce. I generally use sauce No. 1 for this.

MINUTE PUDDING.

One cup of flour and one egg, mixed thoroughly together. Place on the stove in a kettle, one quart of milk; sweeten the batter a little, and also flavor with vanilla to the taste; after the milk boils pour the mixture in, stirring constantly until it thickens, then turn into moulds. Eat with sugar and cream.

TAPIOCA PUDDING.

Pour a quart of warm milk over eight tablespoonfuls of tapioca that has been previously washed through several waters. When it is soft, add three tablespoonfuls of melted butter, five well beaten eggs, also sugar and spice to the taste. Bake in a buttered dish.

APPLE WITH TAPIOCA.

Swell for two hours one large, or two small cups of tapioca, in a quart of water, varying the quantity to suit the size of your dish. Bake until nearly done as many large pared and cored apples as will fill the bottom of a pudding-dish, fill the center where the core came out with sugar, and a small piece of butter; when tender pour over them the tapioca, and bake a full hour.

CHOCOLATE PUDDING.

MRS. BUELL.

Six tablespoonfuls of grated chocolate, ten tablespoonfuls of grated bread-crumbs, one quart of milk. Boil together to the consistency of pap; when cold add one cup of sugar, (brown is the best,) and six eggs, leaving out the whites of two. When baked sufficiently make an icing of the whites of the two eggs, and six tablespoonfuls of sugar and spread over the top, put into the oven a few minutes to brown.

APPLE MERINGUE.

MRS. BUELL.

Two cups of apple-sauce, two cups of sugar, juice and peel of one lemon, one tablespoonful of flour, yolks of five eggs. Bake it and when done, beat the whites of the eggs with two tablespoonfuls of sugar, and spread over the top. Brown in the oven.

APPLE MERINGUE.

Fill a small deep dish half full of stewed apples, or any preserved acid fruit, (peaches are very nice,) and pour over an icing of the beaten whites of six eggs, and six tablespoonfuls of white sugar. Bake slowly in an oven from one to two hours. It can be eaten cold or hot. If the apple is stewed, only let it remain in the oven long enough to cook, and brown the icing nicely.

SNOW PUDDING.

One-half package of gelatine (Cox's) dissolved in cold water, one pint of boiling water added, two cups pulverized sugar, juice of two lemons, then strain it, add the whites of three eggs, beat all very hard for some time until it begins to foam, then put it in moulds, and set it on the ice to congeal. Make a custard of one pint of milk, yolks of three eggs, sweeten, and flavor with lemon to your taste, and pour over the pudding just before it is served.

SUET PUDDING.

Three cups of flour, one cup of suet chopped fine, one cup of milk, one cup of molasses, one cup of raisins (stoned and chopped,) one teaspoonful of saleratus, and one of salt. Tie in a bag, and boil three hours. Eat with wine sauce.

PLUM PUDDING.

Eight eggs, one cup of sugar, one-quarter pound butter, one pound bread-crumbs, one-half pint of flour, one pound raisins, (stoned,) one pound of currants, one teaspoonful baking powder, cinnamon and nutmeg to the taste. Beat the eggs separately, and add the whites last, also add one-half pint of sweet milk. Put in a cloth, and boil four or five hours.

PLUM PUDDING. (Baked.)

Into a quart of boiling milk put a sufficient quantity of grated bread-crumbs to make a tolerably thick batter. Let it stand until lukewarm, when it must be beaten well, and a half pound of butter, and the same quantity of sugar be stirred into it. Add eight eggs well beaten, half a pound of raisins, stoned, cut and floured, half a pound of currants, washed, and dried, and dredged with flour, a quarter of a pound of citron, sliced and floured, also a nutmeg ; a little brandy or wine may be added if preferred. Beat all well together, and pour into a buttered mould or dish, and bake slowly for two hours.

Make a sauce of three beaten eggs, a cup of sugar, and a gill of milk seasoned with lemon. Stir over the fire until it becomes as thick as cream, but do not let it boil, and add two wineglasses of brandy or sherry wine. This pudding may be boiled. Put it in a cloth which must be previously scalded and floured, lay it in a round-bottomed bowl while the mixture is being put in ; leave room for it to swell, and tie up very tightly. Drop into boiling water of which there must be enough to cover the pudding well, and replenish from the tea-kettle as it evaporates. Turn the pudding frequently. When it is done it should be dipped into a pan of cold water, to prevent it adhering to the cloth.

PLUM PUDDING.

MRS. J. QUETTING, BROOKLYN.

One cup of flour, one cup and a half of bread-crumbs, three quarters of a cup of raisins, three-quarters of a cup of currants, three-quarters of a cup of suet, one-half cup of molasses, one-half cup of sweet milk, one-half a teaspoonful of soda, one-half tablespoonful of cinnamon, one-half tablespoonful of cloves and a little salt. Mix well together, and boil four hours.

Wine Sauce.—Two eggs, one cup of sugar, one-half cup of butter, one cup of hot water. Brandy to the taste. Beat the whites of the eggs to a stiff froth and add last.

STRAWBERRY SHORT CAKE.

Take three pints of flour, one and a half cups of shortening, (part butter and part lard,) one teaspoonful of salt, one cup of cold water; cream the shortening until very light, drop through the flour, add the salt, then sprinkle the water in. Turn out on a pastry board, mix it a little with a broad knife, then gently pound with a rolling pin until ready to roll out, roll nearly a half inch in thickness, cut into long squares, or put in round pie pans, and bake quickly. As soon as done split open, butter the inside of both pieces, and sugar liberally, then put a layer of berries on the under crust and sugar, place the top crust on, and sugar the top well. It takes about three pints of berries.

Berry Syrup for same.— One pint of berries, one-half pint of sugar, boil slowly ten minutes, then strain, and set to cool. When you serve the cake it is very nice to pour this over it, or you may serve with cream, or it is very good without sauce of any kind.

BEVIVO. A Very Good Substitute for Charlotte Russe.

One-half box of Cox's gelatine, one pint of boiling water, one tea-cup of sugar, flavored with vanilla, three pints of rich cream, whipped. Put into a large glass bowl, and serve with cut cake.

RICE MERINGUE.

Pick over one tea-cup of rice, wash clean and boil in water until it is soft. When done drain all the water from it, let it get cool, and then add one quart of new milk, the well beaten yolks of three eggs, three tablespoonfuls of white sugar and a litte nutmeg; pour into a baking-dish, and bake half an hour. Let it get cold; then beat the whites stiff, add two great spoonfuls of sugar flavored with lemon or vanilla, and spread it over the pudding, and slightly brown in the oven. Be careful not to let it scorch.

SPANISH CREAM.

Half or a third of a box of Cox's gelatine, one-quarter of a cup of powdered sugar. Dissolve the gelatine in one-half a pint of milk.

Boil one and a half pints of milk, pour it over the gelatine and milk. Beat the yolks of two eggs with a cup of sugar, flavor to the taste, then add to the gelatine and milk. Beat the whites very light with a cup of sugar, and the juice of one lemon; spread it over the top of the pudding, and allow it to stand ten minutes in the oven. Make the day before you wish to use it.

BOHEMIAN CREAM.

Four ounces of any fruit you choose, which has been stoned and sweetened. Pass the fruit through a sieve, and add one and a half ounces of melted or dissolved isinglass, or gelatine to a half-pint of fruit; mix it well together, then whip one pint of rich cream, and add the fruit and gelatine gradually to it. Then pour it all into a mould, set it on ice or in a cool place, and when hardened dip the mould a moment in warm water, and turn it out ready for the table.

CHARLOTTE RUSSE.

Take a half box of Cox's gelatine, put it in a bowl, and pour upon it a half pint of cold water; after standing about ten minutes, pour upon it a half a pint of boiling water. While waiting for this, break into a bowl the yolks of four eggs, beat them very light, then take your gelatine, and put it in a skillet or frying-pan, and place on the stove. When you see it beginning to bubble pour, and stir in very quickly the egg (at this stage it is very apt to curdle, so be particular to stir all the time); when you see it is beginning to thicken remove from the fire, and strain into a large bowl through a wire strainer; then season to your taste with sugar and vanilla. (Of course you must allow in seasoning for the cream that is yet to go in. So make *very sweet*.) Then set away in a cool place, and allow it to congeal. When it becomes firm enough to bear the mark of a spoon, (and not until then,) stir in quickly the froth of three pints of whipped cream. I usually have my cream whipped early in the morning or some time before I am ready to use it, and then there is no detention; as you whip it and the froth rises to the top, skim it off with a spoon, and put on platters. This will make sufficient to fill four or five good sized moulds. Instead of moulds you may take a large, round sponge-cake, turn it bottom upwards, and cut off a slice an inch thick, then remove the whole of the inside, leaving the shell of the cake an inch thick. Pour the mixture in this, put on the bottom slice, and set away in a cool place until ready to serve.

OMELET SOUFLEE.

MISS BARROWS.

Take six eggs, beat the whites and yolks separately until you are worn out, then sweeten and flavor the yolks, mix them with the whites and beat until your patience gives out. Bake in a *very hot* oven until it rises very light, and browns nicely. Eat as soon as done, with sauce.

RICE BALLS.

MISS BARROWS.

Mould rice while hot into balls, or press it into shape in small cups. When cold take out some of the rice from each ball, and place instead some tart sweetmeats. Place all the balls in a flat glass dish, and pour a custard over them.

APPLE CUSTARD.

Pare and quarter six mellow and tart apples, place them in a pan on the stove with a cup of water; as they soften put them in a pudding-dish, and sprinkle sugar over them. Beat eight eggs quite light and sweeten with sugar to the taste, then add three pints of milk, grate in half of a nutmeg, and turn the whole over the apples. Bake about twenty-five minutes.

FRITTERS.

Scald one pint of milk, and stir in flour to make a stiff batter, add a little salt. Beat three eggs separately, stir in just before frying. Fry in hot lard, if it is not boiling hot the fritter will not be light.

POUND PUDDING.

One pound of white sugar, one-half pound of butter, eight eggs, (beaten separately,) one and a quarter pound of flour, and one-half teaspoonful of yeast powder or soda. Beat the sugar and butter well together, then add the yolks of the eggs, and lastly the whites of the eggs and flour. Bake in a cake pan, and serve with sauce.

BAKED FLOUR PUDDING.

One and a half pints of butter-milk, one cup of cream, four eggs, two spoonfuls of saleratus in the milk, flour sufficient to make a batter. If you have no cream take one quart of buttermilk. Eat with cream and sugar or some kind of sauce.

BOILED CUSTARD.

Put on to boil in a kettle three pints of milk with some cinnamon sticks broken into it ; then take two eggs to a pint, breaking them into a bucket (leaving out about two of the whites to whip up and place on top,) beat the eggs up well in the bucket with sugar to the taste, and when the milk boils up pour it in with the egg, stirring all the while, then put some boiling water into the kettle, and place your bucket containing the custard in it, and stir constantly until it begins to thicken (be careful not to allow it to curdle). Then remove it, and place it in a cool place until ready to serve. Have a glass bowl in which you have placed some pieces of sponge cake, with sherry wine sprinkled over it, then strain your custard into this bowl (or you may omit the cake if you wish). Then whip up the whites of the egg, with some currant jelly, and just before serving, with a spoon pile the egg on the top as high as possible. This makes a very pretty dessert.

PUFF PUDDING.

Three eggs, nine tablespoonfuls of flour, one pint of milk, a little salt. Pour the milk scalding hot on the flour, then add the yolks of the eggs beaten very light, and lastly the whites. Bake a half hour in a pudding-dish or pan. Eat with sugar and cream or sauce of some kind.

COCOANUT PUDDING.

MISS ADDIE WILLIAMS.

Grate the meat of half a cocoanut, stir it into a custard made of four eggs to a quart of milk, one tea-cup of sugar. Bake with an under-crust in a buttered dish, in a quick oven for thirty or forty minutes. To be served with the following sauce. One cup of butter, one cup of sugar stirred to a cream, then one cup of wine added slowly; set the bowl containing this into a vessel of hot water for half an hour, do not stir it.

ORANGE PIE.

MISS ADDIE WILLIAMS.

Three large oranges, eight eggs, two coffee-cups of sugar, two cups of cream, one-half cup of butter, three teaspoonfuls of corn starch. Bake as you would lemon pie.

WIGWAM. (A Nice Dessert.)

MISS COLLIER, PHILADELPHIA.

One pound of lady-fingers opened and spread on a dish; cover them with currant jelly, and on the jelly spread meringue, then another layer of lady-fingers, jelly and meringue; make several layers of the cake, jelly and meringue, making each layer a little smaller in order to have it pyramidal form; cover the whole with meringue and put it in the oven a few minutes to brown. The meringue is made of the whites of eggs with sugar beaten in, but do not make it too stiff.

LEMON CUSTARD.

MRS. NYE.

Six tablespoonfuls of sugar, two lemons, and six eggs. Beat the yolks of the eggs with the sugar, beat the whites to a stiff froth and add them, grate in the lemon peel, and squeeze in the juice, then add a small piece of butter, and bake like custard.

AMBROSIA.

MATTIE NYE.

Peel and slice thin some oranges, take out the seeds as you slice them, sprinkle with sugar and grated cocoanut. Fill a glass bowl with the oranges, sugar and cocoanut alternately piling the cocoanut on top. You may also add pineapple if you wish.

RICE PUDDING.

MRS. NYE.

One cup of rice, and three pints of milk cooked until perfectly soft, and stiff. While hot stir in the yolks of four eggs beaten light, and grated rind of one lemon. Beat the whites of two eggs to a froth with eight tablespoonfuls of white sugar, and juice of a lemon. Place this on top of the pudding, and put in the oven to brown.

BOMBAY PUDDING.

To a good sweet custard, add a little butter, a little nutmeg, and a glass of wine. Mix in a grated cocoanut. Line a dish with puff paste, and bake a light brown.

DUTCH BLANC-MANGE.

MISS M. STILLWELL.

To one quart of boiling water, one-half box of Cox's gelatine, juice of two large lemons, two coffee-cups of sugar. When almost cold pour over the beaten yolks of six eggs.

COCOANUT BLANC-MANGE.

MATTIE NYE.

Let one quart of sweet milk come to a boil, then stir in one grated cocoanut, and three even tablespoonfuls of corn-starch, mixed with enough cold water to soften, and sugar sufficient to sweeten. Let this cook three-quarters of an hour stirring occasionally, then take it off the fire, and stir in the beaten whites of four eggs. Pour into a mould and when cold serve with cream.

FRUIT MERINGUE.

MRS. H. IDE, COLUMBUS.

Fill a dish with fruit of any kind, (canned peaches are very nice,) sugar well, and then make a meringue of egg and sugar. My rule is nine tablespoonfuls of sugar to the white of one egg, (of course you must use your own judgment according to the size of your dish,) then pour the meringue over the fruit, put it in the oven, and bake brown. The meringue should be well baked through. Serve with cream, or without anything.

CORN STARCH PUDDING.

Stir three or four tablespoonfuls of starch into a pint of boiling milk, and when quite thick take it from the fire, and set it aside to cool. Then mix with it half a pound of sugar, a quarter of a pound of butter, and eight eggs beaten separately and light, and beat all well together. Season with essence of lemon, put into a pudding-dish, and set in the oven to brown.

FULLER PUDDING.

MRS. C. PORTER.

One cup of molasses, two-thirds of a cup of butter, one cup of water, one teaspoonful of soda, two of ground cloves, one of salt, four even cups of flour. Steam three hours.

Sauce for Same.—One cup of butter, two of sugar, one of wine, two eggs. Stir the butter and sugar together, beat the eggs with the butter and sugar thoroughly, and steam over boiling water until scalding hot. Do not let boil.

ALMOND CUSTARD.

MRS. C. PORTER.

One pint of new milk, one cup of fine sugar, one-quarter of a pound of blanched almonds (pounded), two spoonfuls of rose-water, the yolks of four eggs, stir this over a slow fire until it is the consistency of cream, then remove it quickly, and put it in a pudding-dish. Beat the whites of the eggs to a stiff froth with a little sugar, and spread on the top.

SYLLABUB.

One quart of cream, one gill of wine. the juice of three lemons, the beaten whites of six eggs, and sugar to your taste. Froth these ingredients with a syllabub-churn, and put into glasses. Hand around with cut cake.

ICE CREAM.

MRS. B. WHEELER.

One gallon of cream, one and a half pounds of sugar, two eggs beaten light and mixed with the cream. Strain it and put it in the freezer, stir until done. Break the ice fine and sprinkle salt over it, filling it tightly around the freezer.

LEMON ICE.

MRS. B. WHEELER.

Eight lemons, two quarts of water, one and a half pounds of sugar, whites of four eggs. This will make three quarts to freeze.

PUDDING SAUCE.

No. 1.—Put into a tin-cup two eggs, and one cup of sugar, beat very hard to a stiff froth, have a pan of water boiling on the stove, place the tin-cup containing the egg and sugar in it, stirring constantly until it comes to a boil. Have a piece of butter size of a walnut in a tureen, pour the egg over it, and flavor with wine (sherry), vanilla or both. This can be made early in the morning as it should be cold when eaten. Stir well before using. This is a very nice sauce for plum pudding.

No. 2.—One-half cup of butter, one cup of sugar, yolk of one egg, and a tea-cup of water. Melt the sugar and butter together, then add the egg well beaten and water. Cook a few minutes. Flavor with wine or vanilla.—*Mrs. Adams.*

No. 3.—One-half a pound of sugar, one-half a pound of butter, one tablespoonful of flour, two tablespoonfuls of water. Flavor with sherry wine and nutmeg.—*Mrs. Woodbridge, Chillicothe.*

No. 4.—One cup of powdered sugar, and one-half a cup of butter beaten to a cream, the yolk of one egg beaten and added, then the white of the egg beaten light and also added ; melt over a pan of boiling water, and add a wine-glass of wine.

No. 5.—*Cold Sauce.*—Four ounces of butter, six ounces of sugar, white of one egg. Beat the butter and sugar together very white, then add the egg, beaten light, also a glass of wine and nutmeg.

No. 6.—Boil half a pint of cream, thicken it with a teaspoonful of flour, and put in a large lump of butter. Sweeten to your taste, and when cold add wine or brandy.

No. 7.—Boil some lemon rinds, and a gill of milk together until the milk is flavored, then stir in three well beaten eggs, and sweeten with sugar to your taste. Stir constantly until it is as thick as thin cream, but do not let it boil, and then stir in two wineglassfuls of brandy or sherry wine.

No. 8.—One quart of boiling water, four large tablespoonfuls of white sugar, two of flour, one of butter, one teaspoonful of salt ; nutmeg or cinnamon to the taste. Let the whole boil together for ten minutes, and season with vanilla or wine. Mix the flour with a little cold water before adding to the boiling water.

BRANDY SAUCE. (Hard.)

One-half cup of butter, two cups powdered sugar, one glass of wine (sherry) or brandy, nutmeg. Warm the butter very slightly, then add the sugar, beat to a cream, and then the brandy or wine ; shape into a mould and set in a cold place until wanted, then grate the nutmeg over it.

PUDDING SAUCE.

One and a half cups of sugar, one-half cup of butter, one egg beaten to a froth. When the whole has been beaten together very thoroughly, pour in one great spoonful and a half of boiling water, and let it boil up once, beating it all the time. Then remove from the fire, and flavor with nutmeg and half a wineglass of wine.

CAKES.

FRUIT CAKE.

Two pounds of butter, two pounds of flour, two and a half pounds of sugar, twenty eggs, four pounds of raisins, four pounds currants, two pounds of citron, one spoonful saleratus, spices to the taste, wine and brandy sufficient to make it quite moist; two tea-cups of molasses is a great addition, it keeps it moist. This quantity will make two large cakes. It is better to prepare all your ingredients the day before you wish to make it up.

COMMON FRUIT CAKE.

MRS. H. STURGES.

Two cups of brown sugar, one-half cup of butter, two cups of milk, five cups of flour, two cups of raisins; sometimes I add the yolk of one egg, spice to your taste, or about three tablespoonfuls of cinnamon, one of cloves, and one nutmeg, soda and cream of tarter. If you have sour milk use only soda, which is better.

BLACK CAKE.

One pound of flour, one pound of sugar, one pound of butter, two pounds of currants, two pounds of raisins, one pound citron, twelve eggs, one glass of wine, one glass of brandy, four nutmegs (grated), cinnamon and mace; also may be added a cup of molasses. To make this cake the flour should be scorched a cinnamon color in the oven.

WASHINGTON CAKE.

One pound and three-quarters of flour, one pound of butter, one and a half pounds of sugar, eight eggs, dessert spoonful of soda, one wine glass of brandy or wine, three pounds of raisins, one pint sour cream with the soda in it, and added last. A very nice cake indeed.

CAROLINA CAKE.

Two cups of sugar, one cup of butter, three cups of flour, one-half cup of sweet milk, whites of eight eggs, one teaspoonful of cream of tarter, one-half of soda. Rub the sugar and butter to a cream, put the soda in the milk, and add that, then whip the whites, and add them alternately with the flour; the cream of tarter must be put into the flour. One grated cocoanut added to this makes a very nice cake.

WHITE CAKE.

MRS. H. STURGES.

Three-quarters of a coffee cup of butter, two of sugar, one of milk, not quite four of flour, whites of eight eggs, one teaspoonful of soda in the milk, and two of cream of tarter in the flour. Beat the sugar and butter to a cream, then add the whites of the eggs without beating, and beat very well, then half of the milk, and half of the flour and beat well, then the other half and beat well. Bake one and a half hours.

WHITE MOUNTAIN CAKE.

One pound of sugar, one pound of flour, one-half pound of butter, the whites of eight eggs, one tablespoonful of baking powder in the flour, or two teaspoonfuls of cream of tarter, and one of soda, one cup of sour cream. Bake in layers like jelly cake.

ICING FOR SAME.

One pound powdered sugar, a very small quantity of water to dissolve the sugar, then take the whites of three eggs, and after beating them light, add the sugar. Spread on the cake, and put grated cocoanut between each layer, and over the top, or the cocoanut may be omitted

BRIDE'S CAKE.

One pound of flour, one pound of sugar, three-quarters of a pound of butter, the whites of fifteen eggs; season with nutmeg and lemon.

RAISIN CAKE.

One-half pound of butter, three-quarters of a pound of sugar, four eggs beaten together, one gill of sour cream, one teaspoonful of soda, one wine glass of brandy, one of wine, one pound of raisins, and one of currants.

GOLDEN CAKE.

One tea-cup of sugar, three-quarters of a cup of butter, one-quarter of a cup of sweet milk, yolks of eight eggs, one-half teaspoonful of cream of tarter in the flour, one-quarter of a teaspoonful of soda in the milk, two cups of flour.

SILVER CAKE.

Three-quarters of a cup of butter, two cups of sugar, two and a half cups of flour, one-half teaspoonful of soda, one-half cup of sweet milk, one teaspoonful of cream of tarter in the flour, the juice and grated rind of one lemon, last the whites of eight eggs. It is very well to make these two cakes at one time.

CHOCOLATE CAKE.

MRS. G. JEWETT.

Three-quarters of a cup of butter, four eggs beaten separately, one cup of milk, two of sugar, three cups of flour, four teaspoonfuls of baking powder. Bake in jelly cake-pans.

ICING FOR SAME.

One cup of grated chocolate, one cup of sugar, one-half cup of sweet milk; dissolve the sugar in the milk, put in the chocolate, and boil all together, put on the cake while warm.

COCOANUT CAKE.

One cup of butter, two cups of sugar, one of sweet milk, four of sifted flour, whites of eight eggs, one teaspoonful of soda in the milk, two teaspoonfuls of cream of tarter in the flour, one cocoanut grated. Bake in a large cake-pan.

LEMON CAKE.

Four eggs beaten together, two cups of sugar, two cups of flour, two teaspoonfuls of baking powder, two-thirds of a cup of boiling water, a pinch of salt. This is to be baked in jelly-cake pans. Then take one large lemon (cut the outside rind off), grate it in a dish, stir half in the cake, and half in the icing, which must be prepared in the usual way, keeping out sufficient icing without the lemon to place on top of the cake.

ALMOND CAKE.

One pound of butter, one pound of sugar, one pound of flour, twelve eggs beaten light, two pounds of almonds blanched (by pouring boiling water over them), and pounded in a mortar with rose water. Mix as pound cake. After pouring boiling water over the almonds, remove the skins, and drop them into cold water to keep them white until you are ready to pound them.

POUND CAKE. (No. 1.)

Cream a pound of butter, and beat it with a pound of powdered loaf-sugar. Beat eight eggs separately and light, and add the yolks to the sugar and butter. Stir in the flour and beaten whites alternately. Beat well, and bake in a buttered mould, or small pound-cake pans.

POUND CAKE. (No. 2.)

Two cups of butter, two cups of sugar, two and a half cups of flour, seven eggs beaten separately, nutmeg to season. Beat well, and bake as above.

SPONGE CAKE.

One cup of sugar, one cup of flour, and one tablespoonful of vinegar, and two of water to every three eggs. Use the juice of one lemon instead of vinegar if convenient. Beat the yellows of the eggs very light, then add the sugar and beat well together, then the vinegar and water. After beating the whites to a froth add them, and lastly stir in the flour very gently.

BREAD CAKE.

One pint of bread-dough, one cup of butter, two of sugar, five eggs, one cup of sour cream with a teaspoonful of soda in it, cloves, cinnamon and nutmeg to the taste. Work the butter and dough well together; beat the sugar and eggs together very light, and put into the dough, then the cream and spices. Put it in a pan, and let stand until light.

COOKIES.

Eight cups of flour, three cups of sugar, one cup of butter, one cup of cream, one teaspoonful of saleratus. Mix well, roll out thin and cut.

SUGAR COOKIES.

MRS. B. WHEELER.

Two cups of sugar, one cup of butter, one cup of sour milk, two eggs, one teaspoonful of soda. Mix very soft.

CUP CAKE.

MRS. P. BLACK.

One cup of butter, eight eggs, four cups of sugar, seven cups of flour, two cups of sweet milk, with two teaspoonfuls of soda dissolved in it, and four teaspoonfuls of cream of tarter rubbed well through the flour, add a little salt, and vanilla. Some raisins may be added if you like.

CUP CAKE.

Three cups of sugar, two cups of butter, five cups of flour, three eggs, a little brandy or wine. Beat well, and bake in pans.

CURRANT CAKE.

Three cups of sugar, one-half cup of butter, four cups of flour, five eggs, one cup of milk, one teaspoonful of soda, currants any quantity you please.

CREAM CAKE.

Four cups of flour, three of sugar, one of butter, one of cream, five eggs, and three-fourths of a teaspoonful of soda. Rub the butter and sugar together, mix in the other ingredients, and bake as pound cake.

BUCKEYE CAKE.

One cup of butter, three of sugar, one of sweet milk, six eggs, four cups of flour, one teaspoonful of soda in the milk, two of cream of tarter in the flour (or one tablespoonful of baking powder). Bake as you would sponge cake. This is a very good receipt for jelly cake.

TEA CAKE. (No. 1.)

MRS. STEVENSON.

One cup of butter, two cups of sugar, three eggs, four cups of flour, one-half teaspoonful of soda, three tablespoonfuls of sour milk, spices to the taste. Beat the sugar and butter together, then add the eggs without beating; after mixing well together, put in the milk, and lastly the flour. The batter will be quite soft, add just enough flour to roll out; they will be so soft when cut that it will be necessary to lift them with a knife to put into the pans.

TEA CAKE. (No. 2.)

One cup of sugar, one cup of butter, one cup of cream, one egg, six cups of flour, a half teaspoonful of saleratus, a little nutmeg, and a very small portion of allspice.

JUMBLES.

One cup of butter, one cup of sugar, three eggs (broken into the butter and sugar without beating,) and one nutmeg. Beat very light and add a little flour; they must be made up soft, take out a very small portion on your board at a time, roll with the hand in flour, then in sugar, turn and fasten the ends together, leaving a hole in the center. Bake in a hot oven.

ALMOND JUMBLES.

One pound of butter, one pound of sugar, one and a half pounds of flour, six eggs, leaving out the whites of four. Flavor with nutmeg. Blanch the almonds, chop them up, mix with white sugar, and place on top. One-half pound of almonds in the shell is sufficient.

MACAROONS.

Three eggs, one-half pound loaf-sugar, one pound of blanched almonds, one-quarter pound of bitter almonds. Beat eggs separately to a froth, add the sugar to the yolks, then the whites, and lastly the almonds. Drop on buttered paper, and bake on tins in a quick oven for fifteen minutes until of a pale brown color.

ALMOND CAKE.

MISS MATTIE NYE.

Make a white mountain cake, and put the following mixture between: The yolks of four eggs, and two tablespoonfuls of sugar, beaten light, the whites also beaten light with the same quantity of sugar, and then both mixed together, one-half glass of wine, one tablespoonful of vanilla, one pound of blanched almonds cut fine, and one-half pint of sour cream.

NUT CAKE.

MISS MATTIE NYE.

Two tablespoonfuls of butter, two cups of sugar, one cup of milk, three cups of flour, one teaspoonful of cream of tarter, one-half teaspoonful of soda, one pint of hickory-nut meats, flavor with vanilla.

ROUGH AND READY CAKE.
MISS MATTIE NYE.

One cup of butter, two cups of sugar, one cup of sweet milk, one teaspoonful of soda, two teaspoonfuls of cream of tarter, seven eggs, one pound of raisins, one pound and a half of blanched almonds, one-half pound of citron, not quite four cups of flour.

SEED CAKES.

One pound of sugar, one-half pound of butter, one tea-cup of sour cream, one teaspoonful of soda, one tablespoonful of caraway seeds, flour sufficient to roll out. Cut and bake in a quick oven.

GENTLEMAN'S GINGERBREAD.
MRS. NYE, CHILLICOTHE.

Beat very light one-half pound of butter and one-half pound of sugar, add the yolks of twelve eggs beaten very light, two-thirds of a glass of brandy, one glass and a half of wine, the juice and grated rind of one lemon, one grated nutmeg, two large tablespoonfuls of cinnamon, and six tablespoonfuls of ginger; when well beaten stir in one-half pound of flour, and beat the mixture thoroughly. Spread it very thin on buttered pans, bake in a quick oven, and cut in squares while warm.

SCOTCH CAKE.

Stir to a cream one pound of sugar and three-quarters of a pound of butter; grate the peel of one lemon, and also add the juice, one wineglass of brandy. Separate the yolks and whites of nine eggs, beat them to a froth, and stir them into the cake; then add one pound of flour, and lastly one pound of raisins.

LEMON MIXTURE FOR CAKE.
MATTIE NYE.

Grate two or three lemons, and press out the juice, taking care to remove all the seeds, one coffee-cup of white sugar, two eggs, piece of butter the size of an egg. Beat the sugar and eggs together, add the lemon, and boil until smooth; stirring all the time.

CHICAGO CAKE.

MRS. C. PORTER.

Four cups of flour, three cups of sugar, one cup of butter, one cup of milk, whites of ten eggs, one teaspoonful of cream of tarter, and one-half teaspoonful of soda.

LANCASTER CAKE.

MRS. C. PORTER.

One pint of sour cream, blanch and pulverize one pound of almonds, three eggs, four tablespoonfuls of sugar, vanilla to the taste. Beat the yolks with two tablespoonfuls of sugar; mix the almonds with the cream, beat the whites to a stiff froth with two tablespoonfuls of sugar, and add to the cream. Mix all together; it should be as thick as sponge cake batter. This is to be put between layers of cup or delicate cake, as you would in making jelly-cake.

ICE CREAM CAKE.

MRS. NYE.

One cup of butter, two cups of sugar, one cup of sweet milk, whites of eight eggs, three cups of flour, two teaspoonfuls of baking powder. Bake in jelly-cake pans.

Icing for the above.—One tea-cup of sugar, one-half tea-cup of water, whites of three eggs. Boil the sugar and water together, and when it comes to a boil, stir in the whites of the eggs well beaten, one teaspoonful of citric acid, one teaspoonful of essence of lemon, and one of vanilla.

TO MAKE KISSES.

Beat the whites of eight eggs to a stiff froth, and mix in a pound of powdered white sugar a little at a time. Beat well; flavor with

CRULLERS. (No. 1.)

Two cups of butter, two cups of sugar, two cups of buttermilk, five eggs, one teaspoonful of saleratus, one nutmeg, and any other spices you may like, add flour sufficient to roll well; cut and fry in hot lard.

CRULLERS. (No. 2.)

Beat two eggs well with a tea-cup of sugar, stir in half a teacupful of milk, or cream if you have it, and pour into a pan of flour; make a stiff dough, roll it thin, cut it in shapes, and fry in boiling lard. The more lard there is the less they will soak it up, and it must be hot or they will not be light. Sift powdered sugar over them while they are hot.

CRULLERS. (No. 3.)

MRS. JOHN GRANGER.

Two cups of coffee-sugar, one tablespoonful of butter, three eggs, one pint of buttermilk, one nutmeg, one heaping teaspoonful of soda in the milk, flour sufficient to roll out. Fry in hot lard. (Splendid).

DOUGHNUTS.

Stir into one pint of warm milk a half tea-cup of butter, and the same of lard, flour enough to make a stiff batter, one teaspoonful of salt, and one cup of yeast; set near the stove to rise. When light, work in two and a half cups of sugar, four eggs well beaten, two teaspoonfuls of cinnamon, a little nutmeg; add flour until it is not quite as stiff as bread, knead well; let it rise again very light, roll out, and cut in any shape desired. Fry in hot lard, and sprinkle sugar over them while hot.

DOUGHNUTS.
MRS. H. STURGES.

One cup of cream, good and thick, one cup of sugar, one egg, nutmeg, and a little salt, almost one teaspoonful of soda, and two of cream of tarter, flour enough to enable you to roll out; cut them with a biscuit tin.

SOFT GINGER BREAD.

One cup of butter, one cup of sugar, three cups of molasses, five cups of flour, one and a half cups of sour milk or cream, three eggs, one teaspoonful of soda, one large tablespoonful of ginger, add cloves, allspice and cinnamon to the taste; also citron and raisins if you wish.

SOFT GINGER BREAD. (No. 2.)

Two cups of sugar, one cup of butter, one cup of sour milk or cream, one cup of molasses, four eggs, two teaspoonfuls of soda, one tablespoonful of ginger, nutmeg and cloves.

GINGER SNAPS.

One cup of sugar, one cup of butter, one pint of molasses, one teaspoonful of soda, spices to the taste, flour sufficient to roll well, roll thin and cut.

GINGER SNAPS.
MRS. B. WHEELER.

One cup of molasses, one cup of sugar, one-half cup of butter or lard, one and a half teaspoonfuls of soda stirred in the shortening, one tablespoonful of ginger, one tablespoonful of cinnamon, and last put in three tablespoonfuls of water. Flour sufficient to roll out well.

GINGER SNAPS.
MRS. JOHN GRANGER.

One cup of molasses, one tablespoonful of butter; boil together. Ginger to the taste, and flour sufficient to thicken, roll thin and bake in a moderate oven.

JELLY ROLLS.

Three eggs, one cup of sugar, one cup of flour, one teaspoonful of butter, one teaspoonful of yeast powder. Roll very thin.

Jelly for Roll.—One cup of sugar, one egg, juice of one lemon, one teaspoonful cold water; let it thicken on the stove, stirring all the while. You may either use this jelly, or any other you may prefer.

WAFERS.

Mix together, half a pound of sugar, a quarter of a pound of butter, and six well beaten eggs, with flour enough to make a stiff batter. Beat the batter very smooth, and flavor with lemon or nutmeg. Heat and grease the wafer-irons every time you bake one. Roll up the cake while warm (shape of a horn), and sift powdered sugar over them while they are hot.

MARBLE CAKE.

MRS. C. PORTER.

One cup of butter, two cups of sugar, three and a half cups of flour, three eggs, one cup of milk, two teaspoonfuls of baking powder.

For the Dark.—Take two tablespoonfuls of molasses, one teaspoonful of cloves, one of cinnamon and one of nutmeg. Put this in a teacupful of the above mixture, and then pour the white and dark into the pan in alternate layers.

MARBLE CAKE.

For the White Part.—One-half cup of butter, three cups of white sugar, five cups of flour, one-half cup of sweet milk, whites of six eggs, one teaspoonful of baking powder.

Dark Part.—One-half cup of butter, two of brown sugar, one cup of molasses with one teaspoonful of soda, one cup of sweet milk, yolks of six eggs, and one whole egg, teaspoonful each of cinnamon, cloves and allspice, flour to make a soft batter. Cover your pan first with the white mixture, then a layer of the dark giving it a slight stir with the tip of the spoon, then more of the white and so on until your pan is full; having the top layer of the white **mixture.**

CREAM CAKES.

MISS FARLEY, OF BOSTON.

For the Outside.—Boil together one-half pint of water and two-thirds of a cup of butter; while boiling stir in thoroughly one and a half cups of flour. When cool, add five eggs well beaten, and one-quarter of a teaspoonful of soda. Drop and bake about twenty minutes.

For the Inside.—Boil one pint of milk, and while boiling add two eggs, one cup of white sugar and one cup of flour beaten together; after taking from the fire add a small piece of butter and flavor with lemon or vanilla. Split the cakes and fill.

COCOANUT MACAROONS.

Take equal parts of grated cocoanut and powdered white sugar, and mix the beaten whites of two eggs until they form a thick paste. Bake on buttered paper until of a pale brown color.

TRIFLES.

MATTIE NYE.

One egg to a teaspoonful of sugar, and as much flour as will make a stiff dough. Roll very thin, and cut in such shapes as you wish, and fry in hot lard.

CINNAMON WAFERS.

MISS BARROWS.

One pound of white sugar, one-quarter of a pound of butter, three eggs, one-half teaspoonful of soda dissolved in as little water as possible, two tablespoonfuls of ground cinnamon, and flour sufficient to make stiff; roll very thin and bake quickly.

SAND TARTS.

MRS. C. PORTER.

Five-eighths of a pound of butter, one pound of sugar, three eggs, flour enough to mix very soft. Reserve the whites of the two eggs for spreading over the tops of the cakes. Sprinkle with sugar and cinnamon.

Mrs. H's Scotch Cake Jumbles.

MRS. C. PORTER.

One pound of sugar, three-quarters of a pound of butter, three eggs, one tablespoonful of cinnamon, one-quarter of a teaspoonful of soda. Mix to a soft dough.

ONE EGG CAKE.

MRS. C. PORTER.

One egg well beaten, one and a half tea-cups of sugar, piece of butter size of an egg, one cup of milk, one pint of flour, two teaspoonfuls of cream of tarter, one teaspoonful of soda. Bake a half hour.

Mrs. Taylor's Drop Ginger Cake.

MRS. C. PORTER.

One pint of molasses, one cup of sugar, one cup of butter, one cup of milk, four eggs, two teaspoonfuls of soda, one of cinnamon, one of allspice, two of ginger, and a little over one quart of flour.

SUGAR GINGER BREAD.

MISS CAREY.

One cup of butter, two cups of sugar, one egg, one-quarter of a cup of sour cream, or milk, a dessertspoonful of soda, a teaspoonful of ginger; as much flour as can be stirred in, then knead in a little more; roll out thin, cut and bake in a quick oven.

ICING FOR CAKES.

One and a half pints of boiling water, one and a half tablespoonfuls of gelatine, three and a half pounds of powdered sugar, juice of one lemon. Dissolve the gelatine in the water, add the sugar and lemon. Let it stand a few minutes. This is icing sufficient for two large cakes.

BOILED ICING.

Take one pound of sugar and a half a pint of water, boil it well together until it will drop in strings from the spoon, then pour it over the whites of four eggs beaten to a stiff froth, and beat it until cold; flavor with lemon juice or rose water, and apply with a wet knife.

COLD ICING FOR CAKE.

Take one pound of pulverized sugar; beat the whites of three eggs to a stiff froth, and stir gradually into them the sugar. Beat it well and flavor with lemon, or essence of rose.

ICING.

Whites of four eggs, one pound of pulverized sugar, two teaspoonfuls of starch, (corn), essence of lemon to suit the taste.

JELLIES, CORDIALS AND WINES.

WINE JELLY.

Take one box of Cox's gelatine, pour over it a pint of cold water, (in winter I use a pint and a half of both cold and hot water), after standing about ten minutes pour over it the same quantity of boiling water; stir until the gelatine is entirely dissolved, then add one pint of sherry wine, about two pints of sugar, two lemons, (if small use three,) these I pare throwing away the yellow rind, and slicing the lemon very thin, a handful of cinnamon sticks broken up, and two eggs, and as you want to use the shell of the eggs wash them clean, and break the whites on a plate, (leaving out the yolks,) break up the shells in the whites and beat a little, and stir into the mixture just before putting on the stove. Let it boil up several times then remove, and strain through a flannel bag; which should be standing in a pan of boiling water, and wrung out just before the jelly is put in, (the bag used for this jelly should never be used for any other purpose), and one other thing to be remembered is never stir after putting in the eggs. Let it boil and then strain immediately.

ORANGE JELLY.

Take a pint of orange juice to a pound of sugar, and an ounce of isinglass or gelatine, boil and skim for fifteen minutes. Mix in a little of the grated rind, and when done pour into a mould. About one dozen oranges will make this quantity.

BRANDY PEACHES.

Weigh ten pounds of peaches, take eight pounds of sugar to that quantity, and three pints of water to make a syrup. After the peaches are prepared in lye, put them into cold water until you are ready to put them into the syrup; then boil them in the syrup, one-half your peaches at a time until they look clear and tolerably soft, then take them out carefully with a perforated ladle, one at a time, and place them in your glass jars, and pour over them your brandy. Let them stand some hours until the brandy penetrates, then pour off the brandy, and put equal quantities of it with the syrup, and fill up your jars. You will have a great quantity of syrup which must be boiled down more than half, to almost the consistency of taffy.

To make the lye for removing the skin from the peaches: You take two quarts of wood ashes, and one gallon of water, as soon as it boils throw in a dozen peaches at a time; as soon as the skin commences to peel off, (which will be in a moment or two,) take them out with a skimmer, and drop immediately into a bucket or pan of cold water; scrape each one off with a knife, and drop again into another vessel containing clean, cold water, allowing them to remain until you are ready to cook them in the syrup. They will turn black if kept out of the water. One-half gallon of brandy is sufficient to make a great quantity.

BRANDY PEACHES. (A More Simple Rule.)

Take fresh clingstones, and drop for a minute in boiling lye. Remove from the lye with a perforated ladle, and drop in a bucket of cold water. Wipe with a rough towel to remove the skin, and drop into a syrup prepared in the meantime of half a pound of sugar to every pound of fruit. Let them cook fifteen minutes, and take from the syrup and put on dishes to cool. Boil the syrup down to half, and put an equal part of old peach brandy or French brandy if you wish them very strong. They will be very nice with less brandy.

PEACH MARMALADE.

Pare your peaches, take out the stone, weigh, chop up quite fine, add one-half pound of sugar to every pound of peaches, put in part of the stones, and let simmer for two hours, stirring with great care for fear it should burn.

BLACKBERRY CORDIAL.

MRS. P. BLACK.

To two quarts of juice add one pound of sugar, one-half ounce of cloves, one-half ounce of cinnamon, one-half ounce of nutmeg. Boil twenty minutes, and when cold add one pint good brandy. This is splendid in cases of dysentery.

CHERRY CORDIAL.

Boil and skim the juice, and to every gallon of it take two pounds of sugar. Dissolve the sugar in a *little* water, and when it comes to a boil strain it, and mix with the juice, and to this quantity add a half pint of spirits. Bottle when cold.

BLACKBERRY SYRUP.

Half a pound of blackberry root, and one-half pound of white oak bark, cut into small pieces or pulverized, and boiled in one gallon of water until it is reduced to two quarts, then strain, and boil up with cloves, cinnamon and pepper, and enough sugar to make a thick syrup. Add one gill best French brandy to each quart. Bottle and seal with wax, when it will keep for years. This was used most successfully during the late war, in cases of dysentery.

CURRANT WINE.

Crush the fruit, strain off the juice, put it into a tub, and let it stand three days, removing the scum once or twice a day. Then put it into a keg or barrel, and to each quart of juice add three pounds of the best white sugar, and water sufficient to make one gallon. If you do not like sweet wine reduce the sugar to two and a half pounds, or even less to the gallon. The cask must be full, and the bung left off until fermentation ceases (which is usually from twelve to fifteen days). Fill the cask up daily with water. When fermentation ceases, rack the wine off carefully by a syphon, then cleanse the cask thoroughly with boiling water; return the wine to it, stop it tightly and let it stand four or five months.

BLACKBERRY WINE.

To every gallon of berries, after being well mashed, one quart of boiling water. Let it stand twenty-four hours, then strain, and add three pounds of loaf-sugar to every gallon of juice. Let it stand until it is done fermenting for three or four weeks, with the bung laid on loosely. At the end of that time stop it tightly, and set away for some months, and then bottle it. Strawberry wine is made in the same way, except that no water is added to the juice.

RASPBERRY VINEGAR.

Squeeze the juice from three pints of raspberries, and mix with one pint of the best white vinegar, and a pound of loaf-sugar. Simmer in a jar or pitcher, set in boiling water for an hour, skim it, and bottle when cold. Put a teaspoonful of this into half a pint of water, and it makes a very pleasant drink.

RASPBERRY VINEGAR.

MISS BARROWS.

Pour half a pint of vinegar over four pounds of raspberries, place this in an earthen jar, *cover tight*, and place it in a sunny window for twelve hours. Take it in at night, and put it in the window the following day for another twelve hours. Turn into a flannel bag and let all the juice drain through without pressure. Put one pound of sugar to one pint of juice, boil until the scum rises, skim thoroughly, and then cork up tight in bottles.

STRAWBERRY VINEGAR.

Put four pounds of very ripe strawberries into three quarts of the best vinegar, and let them stand three or four days. Then drain the vinegar through a jelly-bag, and pour on to the same quantity of fruit. Then strain again, and to every pound of liquor add one pound of sugar; bottle and let it stand covered, but not corked, one week. Then cork tightly, and set in a dry, cool place.

TO PRESERVE LEMONS.

MRS. FULTON.

Squeeze the juice from the lemon and put the rind into a brine that will bear an egg. Let them remain from one to six weeks as convenient, then take them from the brine, weigh them, cut in slices and soak for twenty-four hours in fresh cold water. Then put them on the stove in cold water and let them boil several hours until tender. Take pound for pound of sugar, with one-half pint of water to a pound, and cook until the syrup is rich and thick.

Oranges can be done in the same way.

CONSERVED PEACHES.

Pare and cut your fruit, and to each pound of fruit take three-quarters of a pound of loaf-sugar. Boil them until clear, take them out, and drain them slightly, and spread on dishes to dry. Sprinkle a little sugar on them every day, and if any syrup is formed, remove them to fresh dishes. When quite dry, lay them lightly in a jar with alternate layers of sugar. Quinces are nice prepared in the same way.

BLACKBERRY JAM.

To six quarts of ripe berries take three pounds of sugar. Put it into a kettle and boil two hours, stirring frequently. Put in any spices you like or omit them. When cool, put it into a jar, cover with brandied paper, and seal. It will keep for years.

To Make Any Kind of Jelly Quickly.

MISS CHAPMAN.

One pound of sugar to one pint of juice. Heat the sugar as hot as possible without burning or dissolving it (in the oven of the stove). Boil the juice five minutes, add the hot sugar, stir it well, and when it has boiled one minute again, set it off and fill your glasses. Observe the time strictly.

ORANGE JELLY.

MRS. NYE.

Peel and cut up six oranges, be careful to remove the seeds, and thick white skin. Put them into a bowl, and sugar them well. For the jelly take a half a box of gelatine, and pour on it one-half pint of cold water, let it soak one hour, then add one and a half pints of boiling water, and sugar to the taste; flavor with the juice of two lemons Stir until the gelatine and sugar are well dissolved, and then pour it over the oranges. Put into a mold, or break up when cool in a glass dish.

CANNED PEACHES.

MISS COLLIER, PHILADELPHIA.

Take one gallon of water to four pounds of sugar. Mix together and when dissolved have the fruit ready in the cans or jars, and pour the syrup over it. Seal the cans up tight, then stand them in a kettle of cold water, and let the water come to a boil, then boil five minutes. Take them out and set away bottom upwards.

PINEAPPLE PRESERVES.

MISS COLLIER, PHILADELPHIA.

Peel the pineapples, and cut out all the eyes, then grate them, add a full pound of sugar for a pound of fruit. Boil until they form a rich jam. Stir a good deal, then seal up.

CRANBERRY JELLY.

FANNY RUSSELL.

Onepart water, threeparts cranberries, boiled in a porcelain kettle until soft. Strain through a colander, not pressing very hard, and *without again putting on the stove*, stir in two parts sugar. Beat quickly until thoroughly mixed, then pour into your molds.

DRINKS.

COFFEE.

Roast it quickly in the oven of the stove until it is a light-brown color, stirring it constantly, and when half cold stir in the beaten whites of two eggs to every two pounds of coffee. Let it stand until it becomes quite cold and dry, and put away in a tight box for use. When you are ready to boil it, grind and mix with a little cold water, allowing a heaping tablespoonful of coffee and a teacup of boiling water to every person. Let it boil rapidly from twenty minutes to a half hour, in a covered tin-pot stirring it from the sides occasionally. Put in a teacupful of cold water to settle it, and after standing for five or six minutes pour it off carefully into another coffee-pot, and send to table. If coffee is not browned well you cannot have good coffee.

TEA.

Have your tea-kettle boiling, and you can always have a good cup of tea. Scald your tea-pot out first, then put in not quite one teaspoonful to each person, pour a little water out of your tea-kettle upon it, and let it stand two or three minutes where it will keep hot, then fill the pot up with boiling water. In making black tea use the same quantity as for green, put it into a tin-cup, fill it up with boiling water, set it on the stove and let it boil up once, then put it into your tea-pot, and fill up with boiling water. Green and black tea mixed are very good.

CHOCOLATE.

Get the best baker's chocolate, and allow for one quart of water four tablespoonfuls of chocolate; mix it with a little water, and then stir it into your vessel of water. Boil fifteen or twenty minutes, then add one quart of milk, let it all boil together a few minutes, then season with a little nutmeg. The sugar and cream may be added at the table.

DISHES FOR INVALIDS.

BEEF TEA.

Take of lean beef (cut into shreds), one pound, water one quart. Boil for twenty minutes, removing any scum that rises. When it has become cold, strain, and add a little salt and pepper.

Another.—Take half a pound of good steak, cut into thin slices, and spread these in a hollow dish; sprinkle a little salt over them, and pour upon the whole a pint of boiling water. Cover the dish, and place it near the fire for half an hour, then remove to a pan, and boil for fifteen minutes; strain through a fine sieve. The quantity of water is too small for the strength of the tea for invalids, but is sufficient to extract all the soluble parts of the beef, and the tea can be reduced to the proper strength by the addition of boiling water.

ESSENCE OF BEEF.

Take of lean beef, sliced, a sufficient quantity to fill the body of a porter bottle, cork loosely, and place it in a pot of cold water, attaching the neck, by means of a string, to the handle of the pot. Boil for one hour and a half to two hours, then decant the liquid, and skim it. To this preparation may be added spices, salt, wine, brandy, etc., according to the taste of the patient, and nature of the disease.

MUTTON TEA.

Take one pound of good mutton, free from the fat, and cut into thin slices; pour over it a pint and a half of boiling water, in the same manner as directed for beef tea; but it requires to be boiled for half an hour previous to straining. If the invalid desires the addition of barley, an ounce of clean pearl barley, washed, and macerated in boiling water for an hour, may be boiled with the mutton tea, and the undissolved barley separated by straining.

CHICKEN BROTH.

Take a small chicken, free it from the skin, and from all the fat between the muscles, divide it longitudinally into halves; remove the lungs, liver, etc., then cut it, bones and muscles, into thin slices, and put these into a pan with a sufficient quantity of salt; add a quart of boiling water, cover the pan, and simmer slowly for two hours; then strain through a fine sieve.

VEGETABLE BROTH.

Take two potatoes, one carrot, one turnip, and one onion. Slice them and boil in a quart of water for an hour, adding more water from time to time, so as to keep up the original quantity; flavor with salt, and a small portion of pot-herbs, strain. When advisable, a small quantity of mushroon catsup added to this broth greatly improves its taste. This is a good substitute for animal food, when the last is inadmissible.

PANADA.

Stale wheat bread, one ounce; cinnamon one drachm, water one pint. Cover up, and let stand for an hour, beat up, and boil for ten minutes, adding a little grated nutmeg and sugar. Wine may be added if required.

BOILED FLOUR.

Take of fine flour one pound, tie it up in a linen cloth as tight as possible, and after frequently dipping it into cold water, dredge the outside with flour till a crust is formed round it, which will prevent the water soaking into it while boiling. Boil for a long time, and permit to cool, when it will become a hard, dry mass. This is to be grated, and prepared like arrow root. A good diet for children in diarrhea.

TOAST WATER.

Toast thoroughly a slice of stale bread, put it in a jug, and pour over it a quart of water which has been boiled and cooled, and in two hours decant; a small piece of orange or lemon peel put into the jug with the bread improves the flavor greatly. This forms a good drink in febrile affections.

MULLED WINE.

Take a quarter of an ounce of bruised cinnamon, half a nutmeg, (grated), and ten bruised cloves; infuse them in half a pint of boiling water for an hour, strain, and add half an ounce of white sugar. Pour the whole into a pint of hot port or sherry wine. This is a good cordial and restorative in the low stages of fever, or in the debility of convalescence from fevers.

CAUDLE.

Into a pint of thin gruel, put while it is boiling hot, the yolk of one egg, beaten with sugar, and mix with a tablespoonful of cold water, a glass of wine, and some nutmeg. Mix well together. This is a nourishing restorative mixture given during convalescence.

GRUEL.

ST. LOUIS COOK BOOK.

Gruel can be made of corn meal, arrowroot or oat meal. Take about one tablespoonful of either, mix smooth with a little cold water, then pour over it one pint of boiling water, let it cook on the stove for thirty minutes, stirring frequently, add a little salt; if it thickens too much, add more boiling water. You may add a little sugar, nutmeg and a little milk or cream if desired.

OAT MEAL MUSH.

Have some water boiling on the stove, and stir the oat meal into it. Let it boil until thick and well done, and just before lifting put in a little salt. If you put the salt in too soon it will turn it quite dark. Eat with sugar and cream. A splendid diet for children, or indeed for any one.

BRAN.

Get nice clean coarse bran from the mill, and after your breakfast put about five teaspoonfuls into a tumbler, and fill it up with cream, (milk will do if you have no cream,) put a little salt in if you prefer. Most excellent for dyspepsia, or constipation, and will prolong ones life *indefinitely*, and you may possibly live to see your great-great-grand-children.

MEDICAL.

REMEDY FOR DIPHTHERIA.

Chlorate of potassa is a well known means of arresting the progress of diphtheria. A solution should be kept in every family medicine chest, ready to be administered in every suspicious case of sore throat. The solution is made by dissolving half an ounce of the chlorate in a pint of boiling water. It should be preserved in a bottle, closely corked, and when used the bottle should be shaken with sufficient violence to diffuse the crystalline sediments through the water. The dose is a tablespoonful thrice daily.

Remedy for Hoarseness or Loss of Voice.

Dissolve in the mouth a lump of borax, the size of a garden pea, or about three or four grains. If held in the mouth for ten minutes before speaking or singing, it will act like magic.

Receipt for Chronic Diarrhea.

Cinnamon seed one-half ounce, cardamon seed one-quarter of an ounce, carroway seed one-quarter of an ounce, orange peel two ounces, English gentian one ounce, camomile flowers one-half ounce. Put on to the above one quart of old rye whisky. (They must all be ground up first).

A Splendid Remedy for Dysentery.

A dessert spoonful of olive oil every four hours, and an opium pill between, this is the quantity for an adult, of course it must be much less for a child.

CURE FOR EPILEPSY.

Bromide of Potassium six drachms, bromide of ammonia two scruples, bicarb of potash fifteen grains, tincture of columbia two and a half fluid ounces, water three fluid ounces. Mix and take two tablespoonfuls three times a day before each meal in a little water. It is very necessary for any one so afflicted to be careful as to the diet, take his meals regularly, eating nothing between meals, and never to overload the stomach, eat moderately, and of such food as seems best to agree with him; taking the last meal early which should be light; be careful of over-exertion, and taking too much sleep: also keep the bowels open and regular.

A New Treatment for Cancer.

Dr. Hasse, of Berlin, injects with a hyperdermic syringe, pure alcohol, to which one per cent. of ether is added, not into the new growth, but around its edges; thus obliterating he claims the vessels, especially lymphatics, which convey the infection, and causing the atrophy of the growth itself.

A Most Excellent Remedy for Toothache.

Alchohol one ounce, laudanum one drachm, chloroform five drachms, gum camphor one-half drachm, oil of cloves one-half drachm, sulph. ether two drachms, oil of lavender one drachm. Saturate a small piece of cotton, and put into the cavity; be careful not to touch any part of the mouth with it as it is very pungent; put the cotton on the point of some sharp instrument, put it into the cavity, and place a small piece of clean cotton over it.

CHOLERA MIXTURE.

Laudanum, tincture of Rhubarb, and spirits of camphor, equal parts. Begin with thirty drops, taken clear and unmixed, with a little sugar placed in the mouth afterwards. Repeat the dose (after every evacuation) increasing it if the case becomes urgent to sixty drops, (a teaspoonful), or ninety if necessary. No household should be without this remedy, particularly in the summer.

Another Mixture for Same.

Laudanum two ounces, spirits of camphor two ounces, essence of peppermint two ounces, Hoffman's anodyne two ounces, tincture of cayenne pepper two drachms, tincture of ginger one ounce. This is also invaluable. A teaspoonful in a little water, or a half a teaspoonful repeated in an hour afterward in a tablespoonful of brandy. This preparation will check diarrhea in ten minutes, and abate other premonitory symptoms of cholera immediately.

FOR SORE THROAT.

Take a small quantity of chlorate potassa, pour boiling water on it, and let it stand until it takes up all it will, then add old rye whisky equal to the amount of water you used. Add to this tincture of capsicum until the mixture is pretty sharp, and then it is ready for use. This is good for a gargle in all cases of sore-throat and is an excellent remedy for diphtheria, using it both as a gargle and internally. Dose.—One teaspoonful every hour, or when very bad every half hour. Water will only dissolve a certain quantity of potassa. A good rule, is to take a half a pint of water, and when it has absorbed all the potassa it will, pour the water off and add a half a pint of whisky. The capsicum is harmless so there is no danger of getting too much in, but to this quantity I should say add about two tablespoonfuls, which will make it sufficiently hot.

FOR NEURALGIA.

Alcohol one quart, sulphuric ether four ounces, chloroform two ounces, laudanum two ounces, oil of wintergreen one-half ounce, oil of lavender one-half ounce, camphor one-half ounce. Apply with a silk handkerchief. Half this quantity is enough to have mixed at one time, as the chloroform and ether evaporate so quickly.

Another Remedy for Same.

Bathe the parts affected every fifteen or twenty minutes with acetic acid No. 8.

MILK AS A REMEDY.

An article appeared lately in which it is stated on the authority of a very celebrated physician, that in the East warm milk is used to a great extent as a specific for diarrhea. A pint every four hours it is said will check the most violent diarrhea, incipient cholera, and dysentery. The milk should never be boiled, but only heated sufficiently to be agreeably warm, not too hot to drink. Milk which has been boiled is unfit for use. This writer says: "It has never failed in curing in six or twelve hours, and I have tried it at least fifty times. I also gave it to a dying man who had been subject to dysentery eight months, and it acted on him like a charm, he is still living, a hale, hearty man, and now nothing that may hereafter occur will ever shake his faith in hot milk."

Treatment of Scarlet Fever.

Rubbing the body with hogs lard or fat reduces the temperature of the skin. A celebrated German physician recommends to incorporate one or two grammes of carbolic acid, into one hundred grammes of lard, and with this to rub the whole body, excepting the head, two or three times a day. The acid operates to destroy the germs or spores of the disease, the lard softens the skin and reduces the temperature.

RECEIPT FOR PAREGORIC.
DR. WILLS.

Powdered opium two drachms, gum camphor two scruples, oil of anise seed one fluid drachm, whisky one quart, add lastly three tablespoonfuls of honey. Place all in a bottle together, and for one week shake the mixture twice a day; after standing awhile it will become very clear, then pour off into a small bottle what you wish to use from day to day, and set the other away.

CURE FOR CHILLS AND FEVER.
DR. WILLS.

Quinine is the only remedy, and taken in the following manner, will cure successfully: Have twenty grains of quinine put up in five grains powders; after you have had the chill, and the fever has passed off, take one powder (five grains), then in four or five hours take the same quantity again, and so on until you have taken the twenty grains. You will then escape your chill the third day. Before the seventh day comes around (they come on periodically every seventh day) take the same quantity as before just as if you had had a chill. Keep this treatment up for six or eight weeks, and you will be entirely restored. I think will never have a return of ague.

TO BREAK UP A COLD.
DR. WILLS.

When you feel the first symptoms, take a Dover's powder with a glass of hot lemonade or whisky punch, go to bed, wrap up warm, and by morning you will be entirely relieved. In addition the feet should be bathed in hot mustard water.

A Sovereign Remedy for Earache.

DR. WILLS.

As soon as a child complains of earache, give it sufficient syrup of ipecac to vomit it freely. It will act like a charm, and the child will be asleep and free from the pain fifteen minutes afterwards. If a mother will only use this remedy she will save her child from a great deal of suffering, and herself from many sleepless nights. My plan is to give a teaspoonful of ipecac, after waiting ten or fifteen minutes (giving the child in the mean time plenty of water to drink,) if it then does not produce the desired effect, give another spoonful, this last will usually be sufficient.

PEPPER TEA.

Six red peppers broken in small pieces, one pint of boiling water poured over them, one teaspoonful of salt, one-half pint of vinegar. This is a good remedy for sore throat.

REMEDY FOR A COUGH.

Five cents worth of rock candy, five cents worth of gum arabic, five cents worth of licorice, all dissolved in a pint of water over a slow fire. When cold add five cents worth of paregoric, and five cents worth of syrup of ipecac; bottle and take a teaspoonful several times a day.

REMEDY FOR RHEUMATISM.

One-half pint of turpentine, one-half pint of alcohol, one ounce of camphor, one ounce saltpetre, one ounce ammonia, one-eighth of an ounce of cayenne pepper. Shake well before applying.

ORANGES AS A MEDICINE.

"A distinguished physician once said that if his patients would make a practice of eating a couple of good oranges every morning before breakfast, from February until June, his practice would be gone. The medicinal effect of pure fruit acids is excellent upon the physical system.

To Make a Mustard Plaster.

If you wish it to produce irritation immediately, mix some flour and water together quite stiff, spread this on your cloth and then sprinkle dry mustard on it quite thick, place a thin cloth over this and dampen with hot water. If you do not wish to raise a blister, mix the mustard up with the white of an egg and a little water. A poultice made in this way may be kept on an indefinite time without raising a blister.

TREATMENT OF CROUP.

Every mother knows those fearful premonitory symptoms of croup, the hoarse sepulchral cough which is so startling. The child should be at once taken up, its throat and chest rubbed thoroughly before a hot fire with lard and camphor melted together, then a wet compress put on, by folding up a cloth of a half dozen thicknesses, (have it about two or three inches in width,) wring it out of cold water, then pin it on to a piece of flannel, allowing the flannel to extend beyond it on either side at least an inch, pin it securely around the neck placing another piece of flannel or a soft towel out side, entirely excluding the air. If the child is very much oppressed give sufficient ipecac (syrup) to vomit it; these remedies can be used until you have time to secure a physician. If the child continues to be hoarse, continue giving ipecac all the next day every two hours not enough to vomit it, but sufficient to keep the phlegm loose. Another remedy for croup is alum, about one-half teaspoonful of pulverized alum in a small quantity of molasses, repeat the dose every hour until the patient is relieved; or alum dissolved in water, and given in small doses every hour. Onion syrup is also very good for hoarseness in children; put two or three onions in a pan place them in the oven of the stove, let them get thoroughly baked, then squeeze the juice out into a saucer, and to every spoonful of juice put the same of white sugar, and give the child a teaspoonful every hour or oftener if necessary.

CHILDREN'S SORE MOUTH.

Get the pulverized borax, and to about one-third of a teaspoonful of borax, mix about one and a half teaspoonfuls of powdered sugar. Mother's should wash their babies mouths out every other morning with a solution of borax and water, they should keep a bottle of it dissolved all the time, pour a little into a cup, and with a cloth wrapt around the finger and dipped into the solution, wipe the child's mouth out well with it; this will prevent children ever having sore mouths.

Another Remedy for Scarlet Fever.

"Undress the child and put it to bed at the very first sign of sickness. Give it, if it has already fever, sourish warm lemonade, with some gum arabic in it. Then cover the abdomen with some dry flannel. Take a well-folded bed-sheet and put it in boiling hot water; wring it out by means of dry towels, and put this over the whole and wait. The hot cloth will perhaps require repeated heating, according to the severity of the case and its stage of progress. Perspiration will commence in the child in from ten minutes to two hours. The child then is saved; it soon falls to sleep. Soon after the child awakes it shows slight symptoms of returning inclination for food; if necessary give injections of oil, or soap and water, and its recovery will be as steady as the growth of a green-house plant if well treated. If the above treatment is applied in due time under the eyes and direction of a competent physician, it is said that not one in a hundred children will ever die of scarlet fever.

MISCELLANEOUS.

WHITMAN'S TAFFY.

One quart of granulated sugar, one pint of water, three tablespoonfuls of vinegar, one tablespoonful of butter. Cook until thick, (try in water), and when you take off add one tablespoonful of vanilla.

TAFFY.

MRS. A. V. SMITH.

One pint of white sugar, one-half pint of water, one tablespoonful of vinegar, piece of butter size of a walnut, one teaspoonful of vanilla put in just before it is done. Boil twenty minutes after commencing to boil.

CAROMELS.

MISS FANNY RUSSELL.

One cup of hot water, one cup of chocolate (grated), two cups of brown sugar, one-half cup of butter. If the chocolate is not sweet use three cups of sugar. Stir constantly until the mixture hardens, try it as you would ordinary taffy in cold water.

CAROMELS.

MRS. J. FULTON.

Three pounds of brown sugar, one-half pound of grated chocolate, one and a half cups of milk, lump of butter the size of an egg. Boil like taffy.

ANOTHER FOR SAME.

One cup of molasses, two cups of sugar, one cup of milk, one and a half cups of grated chocolate, a piece of butter size of a hickory nut, and flavor with vanilla. Boil like taffy.

MRS. H.'S CANDY.

One pound of white sugar, one-half cup of vinegar, one-half cup of water, one-half teaspoonful of cream of tarter.

EGG-NOGG.

Take the yolks of sixteen eggs, and twelve tablespoonfuls of pulverized loaf-sugar, beat them to the consistency of cream; to this add two-thirds of a grated nutmeg, and beat well together; then mix in a half pint of good brandy or Jamaica rum, and two wine glasses of Madiera wine. Have ready the whites of the eggs beaten to a stiff froth, and beat them into the above described mixture. When this is all done, stir in six pints of good rich milk. There is no heat used. Egg-nogg made in this manner is digestible and will not cause headache. It makes an excellent drink for debilitated persons, and a nourishing diet for consumptives.

EGG-NOGG. (No. 2.)

Beat separately the yolks and whites of six eggs, stir into the yolks sufficient powdered loaf-sugar to make it pleasantly sweet, beat them until very light, and flavor with a little lemon-juice, and nutmeg. Beat in six tablespoonfuls of brandy. Boil a quart of thin cream or new milk. Fill the goblets half full of the sugar and eggs, after stirring in the beaten whites just before putting into the glasses. Put a teaspoon in each goblet, and place them on a waiter so they can be distributed immediately after the milk is poured in. Pour the boiling milk into a pitcher, and fill up the goblets with it as you hand them around. Stir the milk and egg well together before drinking.

ROMAN PUNCH.

Grate the yellow rinds of two lemons and one orange on a pound of sugar; squeeze over the juice and let it stand until well dissolved. Strain and add half a bottle of champagne, and the beaten whites of four eggs. It is nice frozen, but may be served without anything else than a little finely broken ice.

COTTAGE CHEESE.

Take a pan of clabber, pour off the whey, and put the clabber into a pointed muslin bag to drain. Let it drain twelve hours; then put the curd into a dish, and mash it until very smooth with a spoon, pouring over it some rich cream until the consistency of thin mush. Season with salt to your taste, and set it away in some cool place until tea time. Serve in a glass dish and sprinkle a little pepper over the top.

SOAP.

To one box of concentrated lye take three gallons of rain water, and four and a half pounds of grease; boil two hours and ten minutes, then add one-half pint of salt, then let it boil thirty-five minutes. Stir in gradually one-half gallon warm rain water; draw the fire away from under it, and let it stand in the kettle over night.

SOFT SOAP.

Take seventeen pounds of potash, pour on it a bucket of warm water, add from twenty to twenty-two pounds of grease, then another bucket of warm water. Stir it up, and as it thickens, add water by degrees until the barrel is full. An old brine barrel is the best to use.

HARD SOAP.

Ten pounds of soda-ash, five pounds of unslacked lime, fifteen gallons of soft water. Put it all into a boiler, and stir until it is dissolved well. Boil one hour then pour it off into a tight barrel. When well settled dip it off clear, and to every gallon of lye, add ten pounds of grease. The soap may be finished in three hours.

To Make White-wash that will not Rub Off.

Mix up half a pail full of lime and water ready to put on the wall; then take one gill of flour and mix it with water; then pour on it boiling water sufficient to thicken it; pour it while hot into the white-wash; stir all well together, and it is ready for use.

TO REMOVE RUST FROM STEEL.

Cover the steel with sweet oil well rubbed on. In forty-eight hours rub with finely powdered unslacked lime until the rust disappears.

TO CLEAN MARBLE.

Take two parts of soda, one part of pumice-stone, and one-part finely powdered chalk; sift through a fine sieve, and mix with water. Rub over the marble, and wash off with soap and water.

TO CLEAN PAINT.

Squeeze flannel nearly dry out of warm water, and dip in whiting and apply. With a gentle rubbing it will remove grease and other stains. Wash in warm water, and rub dry with a soft cloth.

CURE FOR FELONS.

Boil up in any iron vessel of sufficient capacity, (say four or six quarts,) enough yellow dock root to make a strong liquor. When sufficiently boiled, and while the liquor is as hot as can be borne by the hand, cover the kettle with a flannel cloth to keep in the heat and steam, hold the hand or finger affected under the cloth, and in the steam, and in five minutes the pain will cease. If it should return, heat the liquor, and do as before.

TO REMOVE PAINT.

Chloroform will remove paint from a garment or elsewhere, when benzine or bisulphide of carbon fails.

TO CLEAN CARPETS.

To one gallon of water, add two tablespoonfuls of spirits of hartshorn. Wring out canton flannel cloths in this mixture, and rub the carpet with the damp cloth. See that the cloth is not too wet, and dry the carpet off with a dry cloth.

TO DESTROY VERMIN.

Hot alum water will destroy red or black ants, or any other insects. Take two pounds of alum, and dissolve it in three or four quarts of boiling water. Let it stand on the fire until the alum disappears, then apply it with a brush while nearly boiling hot. Lyon's roach powder is also very good; it can be obtained at almost any drug store. It will exterminate the small red ants completely.

GLOSS FOR STARCH.

Take two ounces of gum arabic powder, put it into a pitcher, and pour over it a pint of boiling water (according to the degree of strength you desire), and then having covered it let it stand all night. In the morning pour it carefully from the dregs into a clean bottle, cork it and keep it for use. A tablespoonful of gum water stirred into a pint of starch that has been made in the usual manner will give to lawns (either white or printed) a look of newness, when nothing else can restore them after washing. This will also give sufficient gloss to gentleman's shirt bosoms.

AMMONIA FOR HOUSE-CLEANING.

For washing paint put a tablespoonful in a quart of moderately hot water, dip in a flannel cloth, and with this merely wipe off the wood work, no scrubbing is necessary. For taking grease-spots from any fabric, use the ammonia nearly pure, and then lay white blotting paper over the spot, and iron it lightly. In washing laces, put twelve drops in a pint of warm suds. To clean silver, mix two teaspoonfuls of ammonia in a quart of hot soap-suds, put in your silver, and wash it, using an old nail brush for the purpose. It will also clean hair brushes beautifully, simply shaking the brushes up and down in a mixture of one teaspoonful of ammonia to one pint of hot water; rinse them with cold water, and stand them (bristle down) in the wind, or in a hot place to dry. For washing finger marks from looking glasses or windows, put a few drops of the ammonia on a moist rag, and make quick work of it. If you wish your house-plants to flourish put a few drops of the spirits in every pint of water you use in watering. It is good to cleanse the hair, always rinse it off with pure water. It should be purchased by the pound or half pound, as in that way it can be gotten much cheaper.

To Prevent Blue from Fading.

MRS. H. STURGES.

To one gallon of tepid water put one tablespoonful of salt, and the same of sugar of lead. Put in whatever you want to wash and let it soak fifteen or twenty minutes. Then wash and *boil* if you choose.

A Good Way to Wash Black Calico.

Make a kettle of flour starch, allow it to cool sufficiently to bear the hand, then pour it over your calico. Let it stand a short time, wash out thoroughly, then rinse in two clear waters, hang up to dry, and it will look as well as ever.

To Prevent Calico from Fading.

When a calico needs washing dip it in salt water, and let it dry before washing. Once is sufficient, and should be done the first time it is washed.

TO PRESERVE EGGS.

One pint of unslacked lime, one pint of salt, one gallon of water, pack the eggs in stone jars, and after the mixture has settled, pour it over them. Set them where they will not freeze; they will keep for months, and be as fresh as when first put up. Be careful to always select the freshest and nicest eggs you can for putting up.

Cement for Broken China.

Take a very thick solution of gum arabic, stir into it Plaster of Paris until it is a thick paste, apply it with a brush to the fractured edges, stick together, and in three days it cannot be broken in the same place.

TO CLEAN BOTTLES.

Wash the bottle, then cut a raw potato in small pieces, put them into it with a little cold water, shake well, rinse them out, and they will be very clear.

WHITENING THE HANDS.

Take a cake of brown Windsor soap, scrape it in flakes, add one tablespoonful of cologne, one of lemon juice; mix thoroughly, put into a mould and allow to dry.

TO CLEAN MARBLE.

Take a flannel cloth, dampen it, then dip it in soda and rub it on the marble. Then wash off with clear rain water.

CLEANING SILK.

Pare three Irish potatoes, cut into thin slices, and wash them well. Pour on them a half pint of boiling water, and let it stand until cold ; strain the water, and add to it an equal quantity of alcohol. Sponge the silk on the right side, and when half dry, iron it on the wrong side. The most delicate colored silks may be cleansed by this process, which is equally applicable to cloth, velvet, or crape. A black kid glove boiled in water until it becomes a kind of soft glue, and sponge the silk with it, ironing it on the wrong side is a very good way too. There is an article called soap bark, which can be procured at the druggists' which is splendid for any kind of black woolen goods, making them as fresh as when new.

TO CLEAN STRAW MATTING.

Never use soap on matting. When you want to clean it, wash with a cloth dipped in clean salt and water. This prevents it from turnning yellow. After washing wipe dry at once.

HINTS TO YOUNG LADIES.

"FROM THE UGLY-GIRL PAPERS."

"Two simple chemicals should appear on every toilet-table : the carbonate of ammonia and powdered charcoal. No cosmetic has more frequent uses than these. The ammonia must be kept in glass with a glass stopper from the air. French charcoal is preferred by physicians, as it is more finely ground, and a large bottle of it should be kept on hand. In cases of debility, and all wasting disorders it is valuable. To clear the complexion, take a teaspoonful of charcoal well mixed in water or honey for three nights, then use a simple purgative to remove it from the system. It acts like calomel with no bad effect, purifying the blood more effectually than any thing else. But do not omit the aperient, or the charcoal will remain in the system. After this course of purification, tonics may be used."

FOR THE TEETH.

"A very agreeable dentrifice is made from an ounce of myrrh in fine powder, and a little powdered green sage, mixed with two spoonfuls of honey. The teeth should be washed with it every night and morning. Spite of all that is said against it, charcoal holds the highest place as a tooth-powder. It has the property, too, of opposing putrefaction, and destroying vices of the gums. It is most conveniently used when made into paste with honey."

AN INDISPENSABLE POWDER.

A trouble scarcely to be named among refined persons is profuse perspiration, which ruins clothing and comfort alike. For this it is recommended to bathe frequently, putting into the water a cold infusion of rosemary, sage or thyme, and afterward dust the undergarments with a mixture of two and a half drachms of camphor, four ounces of orris-root, and sixteen ounces of starch, the whole reduced to impalpable powder. Tie it in a coarse muslin bag, (or one made of flannel is better if you wish to use it on the flesh.) and shake it over the clothes. This makes a very fine bathing powder."

TO KEEP THE HAIR IN CRIMP.

"Ladies are annoyed by the tendency of their hair to come out of crimp or curl while boating, or horse-back riding. Apply the following bandoline before putting the hair in papers or irons: A quarter of an ounce of gum-tragacanth, one pint of rose-water, five drops of glycerine; mix and let stand over night. If the tragacanth is not dissolved, let it be for a half a day longer; if too thick add more rose-water, and let it be for some hours. When it is a smooth solution, nearly as thin as glycerine, it is fit to use. This is excellent for making the hair curl. Moisten a lock of hair with it, not too wet, and brush round a warm curling-iron, or put up in papillotes. If the curl comes out harsh and stiff, brush it round a cold iron or curling-stick."

POWDER FOR THE SKIN.

"If young ladies *will use powder*, the most harmless is refined chalk, powder is often a protection and comfort on long journeys, or in the city dust. If the pores of the skin must be filled one would prefer clean dust to begin with. A layer of powder will prevent freckles and sun-burn when properly applied. In all these cases it is worth while to know how to use it well. The skin should be as clean and cool as possible to begin. A pellet of chalk, without any poisonous bismuth in it, should be wrapped in coarse linen, and crushed in water, grinding it well between the fingers. Then wash the face quickly with the linen, and the wet powder oozes in its finest state through the cloth, leaving a pure white deposit when dry. Press the face lightly with a damp handkerchief to remove superfluous powder, wiping the brows and nostrils free. This mode of using chalk is less easily detected than when it is dusted on dry."

TO REMOVE FRECKLES.

"Take finely powderrd nitre (saltpetre), and apply it to the freckles by the finger moistened with water and dipped in the powder. When perfectly done, and judiciously repeated, it will remove them effectually without trouble. Rough skins from exposure to the wind in riding, rowing or yachting trouble many ladies who will be glad to know that an application of cold cream or glycerine at night, washed off with fine carbolic soap in the morning, will render them presentable at the breakfast-table. Another method is to rub the face, throat and arms well with cold cream or pure almond oil before going out. With this precaution one may come home from a berry party, or a sail without a trace of that ginger-bread effect too apt to follow these pleasures."

PREPARATION FOR ROUGH SKIN.

"A delicate and effective preparation for rough skins, eruptive diseases, cuts or ulcers, is found in a mixture of one ounce of glycerine, half an ounce of rosemary-water, and twenty drops of carbolic acid. In those dreaded irritations of the skin, occuring in summer, such as hives or prickly heat, this wash gives soothing relief. A solution of this acid, say fifty drops to an ounce of the glycerine, applied at night, forms a protection from musquitoes. Use the pure crystalized form it is far less overpowering in its fragrance than the common sort, Those who dislike it too much to use at night, will find the sting of the bites almost miraculously cured, and the blotches removed by touching them with the mixture in the morning. Babies and children should be touched with it in a reduced form. Two or three drops of otter of roses in the preparation will improve the smell so as to render it tolerable to human beings though not so to musquitoes."

A SPLENDID HAIR TONIC.

"A strong tincture for the hair is made by adding half an ounce of oil of mace to a pint of deoderized alcohol. Pour a spoonful or two into a saucer; dip a small stiff brush into it, and brush the hair smartly, rubbing the tincture well into the roots. On bald spots, if hair will start at all, it may be stimulated by friction with a piece of flannel until the skin looks red, and rubbing the tincture into the scalp. This process must be repeated three times a day for weeks. When the hair begins to grow, apply the tincture once a day until the growth is well established, bathing the head in cold water every morning, and briskly brushing it to bring the blood to the surface."

A Simple and Harmless Hair Dye.

"It is said that the water in which potatoes have been boiled with the skins on forms a speedy and harmless dye for the hair and eyebrows. The pareings of potatoes before cooking may be boiled by themselves, and the water strained off for use. To apply it the shoulders should be covered with cloths to protect the dress and a fine comb dipped in the water drawn through the hair, wetting it at each stroke, until the head is thoroughly soaked. Let the hair dry thoroughly before putting it up. If the result is not satisfactory the first time, repeat the wetting with a sponge, taking care not to discolor the skin of the brow and neck. No hesitation need be felt about trying this, for potato-water is a safe article used in the household in a variety of ways. It relieves chilblains if the feet are soaked in it while the water is hot, and is said to ease rheumatic gout."

"Never use a fine comb to the head, but keep the scalp clean with a solution of ammonia and water, used several times a week, and then give the head a thorough brushing afterwards. A child's head especially is too tender for the use of a fine comb. The proportions are two or three spoonfuls to a basin of water. Apply with a brush and dry well with a soft towel."

REMEDY FOR CORNS.

"When corns are troublesome make a shield of buckskin leather an inch or two across, with a hole cut in the center the size of the corn; touch the exposed spot with pyroligneous acid which will eat it away in a few applications. Besides this a strong mixture of carbolic acid, and glycerine is good, say one-half as much acid as glycerine. Turpentine may also be used for corns and bunions. A weaker solution of carbolic acid will heal soft corns between the toes. A French medical journal reports the cure of the most refactory corns by the morning and evening application with a brush of a drop of a solution of the perchloride of iron. It states, that after a fortnight's continued application, without pain, a patient who had suffered martyrdom for nearly forty years was entirely relieved."

FOR CUTANEOUS ERUPTIONS.

"Those who have the misfortune to contract cutaneous disorders, or from scorbutic affections or the fumes of certain medicines, each and any of which are liable to produce roughness and inflamation of the skin, will be glad of a speedy and certain cure for their affliction. It is a wash of sulphurous acid (not sulphuric) diluted in the proportion of three parts soft water to one of the acid, and used three or four times a day until relieved. Sub-rosa all parasites on furniture, human beings or pets are quickly destroyed by this application."

A Remedy for Moth or Hepatic Spots.

"They are a sign of deep seated disease of the liver. Taraxacum, the extract of dandelion root, is the standing remedy for this, and the usual prescription is a large pill four nights in a week, some times for months. To this may be added the free use of tomatoes, figs, mustard-seed, and all seedy fruits and vegetables, with light boiled meats, and no bread but that of coarse flour. Pastry, puddings of most sorts, and fried food of all kinds must be dispensed with by persons having a tendency to this disease It may take six weeks or even months to make any visible impression on either the health or the moth patches, but success will come at last. One-third of a teaspoonful of chlorate of soda in a wine-glass of water, taken in three doses before meals, will aid the recovery by neutralizing morbid matters in the stomach. There is no sure cosmetic that will reach the moth patches. Such treatment as described, such exercise as is tempting in itself, and gay society, will restore one to conditions of health in which the extinction of these blotches is certain."

COLOGNE.

"A fine cologne is prepared from one gallon of deoderized alcohol, to it add one ounce of oil of lavender, one ounce of oil of orange, two drachms of oil of cedrat, one drachm of oil of neroli, or orange flowers, one drachm of oil of rose, and one drachm of ambergris. Mix well, and keep for three weeks in a cool place.

COLOGNE.

MRS. S. GILBERT.

White whisky one gallon, attar of rose ten drops, musk ten grains, oil of lavender one-half ounce, oil of lemon one-half ounce, oil of bergamot one-half ounce, four Tonka beans cut fine. Let it stand ten or twelve days, shaking it daily.

COMMON COLOGNE. (To Use as a Toilet Water.)

"Oil of bergamot, lavender and lemon each one drachm; oil of rose and jasmine each ten drops; essence of ambergris ten drops, spirits of wine one pint. Mix and keep well closed in a cool place for two months, when it will be fit for use."

COLD CREAM.

"Melt together two ounces of oil of almonds, and one drachm each of white wax and spermaceti; while warm add two ounces of rose-water, and orange flower water half an ounce. Nothing better than this will be found in the range of toilet salves."

Receipts Sent in too Late for Classification.

ENGLISH PLUM PUDDING.
MRS. A. PALMER.

One pound of beef suet, (chop fine), one pound of flour, one pound of currants, one pound of raisins (stoned), one nutmeg, one dozen eggs, one-quarter pound of citron, one small teaspoonful of salt, one-half pint of sweet milk. After mixing well the above ingredients, put into buttered bowls; dip a cloth into boiling water and sprinkle well with flour. Tie the cloths carefully over the bowls to prevent the water from getting into the pudding. Put the bowls into boiling water which must be kept boiling for six hours.

TAPIOCA CREAM.
MISS FARLEY, BOSTON.

Soak three tablespoonfuls of tapioca in water over night. Stir this into one quart of boiling milk, and just before taking from the fire, add the beaten yolks of three eggs, one cup of sugar and a little salt, add the flavoring before cooling. Just before serving heap on the whites of the eggs beaten together with some sugar; a little cream and wine to flavor.

BOSTON BROWN BREAD.

MISS FARLEY.

One coffee-cup of Indian meal, one of rye flour, one-half teacupful of molasses, little less than one pint of milk, one-half teaspoonful of saleratus stirred into the molasses, a little salt. Steam four and a half hours, then place in the oven and brown.

MIXED BREAD.

Take one quart of corn meal, and pour boiling water over it until it is well scalded. When cool enough to bear the hand in it, put in half a cup of molasses, half a pint of yeast, and two quarts of brown flour. Knead well, let it rise, then bake in a steady oven four hours at least. Bake slowly at first.

BOILED BREAD.

MRS. NYE.

(To be eaten warm, with roast meats, at dinner). Two cups of brown flour, two cups of corn meal, one cup of molasses, one quart of sour milk, one teaspoonful of soda. Boil in a mould three hours closely covered.

BRIDGET CAKE.

Take as much dough as you would for a loaf; makes no difference whether it is sponge or after it is first worked. One cup of butter, two cups of brown sugar, four eggs, one cup of raisins, one cup of currants, one tablespoonful of cinnamon, one of cloves, one grated nutmeg, flour enough to stiffen. Let it rise and then bake.

CHOCOLATE ICE.

MRS. NYE.

Take one quart of milk, one-quarter of a quart of chocolate grated, yolks of five eggs. Let it boil, and when cool put into it sugar and vanilla to taste and freeze.

FROZEN PEACHES.
ST. LOUIS COOK BOOK.

Take soft ripe free-stone peaches, peel and smash them through a colander, sweeten very sweet as the freezing makes them lose some sweetness. Then to make ice cream, add equal quantities of cream, with sugar sufficient for both. All fruits can be made in the same way, adding more or less sugar.

STRAWBERRY ICE CREAM.
ST. LOUIS COOK BOOK.

Make a boiled custard of one quart of milk, one teaspoonful of corn starch, two eggs, one cup of sugar; press three pints of strawberries, or as many more as you please through a sieve; make the juice very sweet, add it, with one quart of cream, one cup of sugar, the whites of two eggs well whipped, to the custard, just as you put it into the freezer. This makes one gallon of cream.

LINIMENT FOR SPRAINS.
MRS. A. PALMER.

One ounce oil of wormseed, one ounce of hemlock, one ounce of sassafras, one ounce of cedar, one ounce of red pepper, one ounce gum camphor, three pints of alcohol. This liniment is good for man or beast.

ADDITIONAL RECEIPTS.

The following receipts came after the book had gone to press, consequently they are not paged nor indexed:

KATE'S LEMON PIE.

MRS. MEREDITH, OMAHA.

Pear the yellow rind from one lemon, then grate the remainder, put it in a bowl and add water to make one-half pint. Take the white of one egg and yolks of four, beat the eggs and add three-quarters of a cup of sugar, mixed with one tablespoonful of butter and an even tablespoonful of flour; mix like cake, then add the lemon and water. Make a nice crust, and bake it (first prick it to keep from puffing up). Put the mixture quickly on it and place in the oven until done. When baked spread over it the whites beaten with a little sugar, flavored with any extract you prefer, place again in the oven and dry a few moments. If the lemons are small use two.

CATSKILL PUDDING.

MRS. MEREDITH.

Two eggs, one tablespoonful of butter, one tablespoonful of sugar, one-half teaspoonful of salt, two teaspoonfuls baking powder, sifted into a quart of flour. Drain the syrup off of fruit, (strawberries are excellent,) mix the fruit in the batter, and steam or boil in a mould two hours. Sweeten the juice and pour over when serving. Cream also used with it after the juice is put on makes it very nice.

BAKED APPLE DUMPLING.

MRS. MEREDITH.

Core and pare the apples, put some sugar inside. Make a crust as for baking powder biscuit, only use more shortening, roll the crust thin, and roll each apple in a piece; put them in a pan, and when the crust gets a little baked pour over the dumplings hot water in which sugar and butter are melted, and let them bake well (say about one hour.) There should be a juice around it when done. Eat with cream. You can make the crust of bread dough if you wish.

ENGLISH PUDDING.
MRS. H., OMAHA.

One cup of sweet milk, one cup of chopped suet, one cup of chopped raisins, one cup of molasses, three cups of flour, one teaspoonful of soda, one teaspoonful of cinnamon, one of cloves; steam in a floured bag four hours.

COCOANUT PIE.
MISS MILLS, OMAHA.

Scald one pint of cream or milk, stir into it while on the fire the beaten yolks of two eggs, and one cup of grated cocoanut; watch closely for fear it will curdle, add a little salt, and sugar to the taste. If the milk is not rich add a piece of butter. When baked spread icing over the top.

FLUMMERY.
MRS. H., OMAHA.

Take one cup of tart jelly, one cup of sugar, the white of one egg, beat the whole hard for fifteen minutes. Eat with cream.

ROLLY POOLY PUDDING.
MRS. H., OMAHA.

Make a paste of one-half tea-cup of butter, one quart of flour, two teaspoonfuls of yeast powder, and water sufficient to roll it out, roll it into a piece a half yard long and six inches wide, spread on it any kind of jam or stewed fruit, roll it up, wrap a cloth around it, and steam for two hours.

SAUCE.

One grated lemon, one cup of sugar, one-half cup of butter, one pint of boiling water, one teaspoonful of flour.

GINGER BREAD.
MRS. M.

One pint of N. O. molasses, one-quarter pound of butter, three eggs well beaten, one tablespoonful of soda or saleratus dissolved in one-half cup of warm water; make a batter like cake by stirring in flour to the proper consistency.

ADDITIONAL RECEIPTS.

FRUIT CAKE.
A LADY IN OMAHA.

One cup of butter, two cups of brown sugar, five eggs, four cups of flour, one cup of sour cream, one teaspoonful of soda dissolved in the cream, one pound of stoned raisins, one pound of citron cut fine, one pound blanched almonds, one teaspoonful of mace, one each of cloves, allspice and cinnamon, one nutmeg. Bake two hours in a slow oven.

HICKORY NUT CAKE.

One cup of butter beaten to a cream, two cups of powdered sugar, one cup of sweet milk, one small teaspoonful of soda in the milk, two teaspoonfuls of cream of tarter in the flour, one cup of corn starch, two cups of flour, the whites of six eggs, one tea-cup of hickory nut meats.

FEATHER CAKE.
MRS. H., OMAHA.

One egg, one cup of sugar, one tablespoonful of butter, one and a half cups of flour, one and a half cups of milk, one teaspoonful of yeast powder. Flavor to the taste.

SNOW CAKE.
MRS. H., OMAHA.

One-third of a tumbler of corn starch, fill up the tumbler with flour, one and a half tumblers of powdered sugar, whites of ten eggs beaten stiff, one even teaspoonful of cream of tarter ; mix the flour, corn starch and cream of tarter together, put it in with the egg, and add one teaspoonful of vanilla and one of lemon. Bake in a quick oven three-quarters of an hour.

WHITE SPONGE CAKE.
MRS. P., OMAHA

Whites of ten eggs, one coffee-cup of flour, one and a half cups of powdered sugar, juice of a small lemon, one-half teaspoonful of cream of tarter, one teaspoonful of extract of lemon. Put the sugar, cream of tarter and flour together, then stir in the eggs, and bake at once.

FRENCH ROLLS.
MRS. H., OMAHA.

Two teaspoonfuls of lard rubbed into two quarts of flour, one tablespoonful of sugar, dessert spoonful of salt, one pint of warm milk, one-half teaspoonful of yeast; let rise, make out in rolls, let rise again and bake.

CORN GRIDDLE CAKES.

One quart of sweet milk, one-half teaspoonful of salt, three eggs, one pint of corn meal, one tablespoonful of molasses or sugar.

WAFFLES. (Excellent.)
MRS. MEREDITH.

Four eggs, one pound of flour, one pint of milk, four tablespoonfuls of yeast, two ounces of butter, one teaspoonful of salt. Beat the eggs to a froth, put the butter into the milk, warm it until the butter melts, then let it cool, and add the milk, then the eggs and flour, stir in the salt and yeast; let stand until light. Pour on well greased waffle-irons, bake on both sides by turning the irons; butter and serve hot.

TO FRY OYSTERS.
MRS. H., OMAHA.

Drain your oysters and wipe them dry, have ready for one can, five beaten eggs and some rolled crackers, dip the oysters first in the egg, then in cracker, do this twice, then put them to fry on a griddle with some lard, add salt and pepper.

PANNED OYSTERS.
MRS. H., OMAHA.

Drain your oysters perfectly dry in a colander, then put into a frying pan a half a tea-cup of butter. When hot throw in your oysters, and salt and pepper them; toss them about in the pan, and serve hot; adding a little mace. Do not use the liquor at all as there will be plenty from the heating.

CORN BREAD.
MRS. C. W. POTWIN.

One quart of sweet milk, one quart of sifted meal, two teaspoonfuls of cream of tarter dissolved in cold water, one teaspoonful of salt, one tablespoonful of melted butter, three eggs well beaten together, one teaspoonful of soda dissolved in hot water, and put in last.

CONTENTS.

Soups.
	Page.
Vegetable Soup	7
Oyster Soup, without Oysters	7
Pea Soup	8
Tomato, (2)	8
Oyster Soup	8
To Prepare Stock for Soup	9
Vermicelli Soup	9
Noodle Soup	9
Rich White Soup	10
Rich Brown Soup	10
Chicken Soup	10

Fish.
Baked Shad or White Fish	11
To Boil Salt Shad or Mackerel	11
Fried Oysters	12
Scalloped Oysters	12
Oyster Pie	12
Spiced Oysters	12
Scrambled Oysters	13
Cod Fish Balls	13

Eggs.
Omelet No. 1	13
Omelet No. 2	14
Omelet No. 3	14
Scrambled Eggs	14
Scrambled Eggs, more simple	14
Omelet	15

Sauces for Meats.
Drawn Butter	15
Egg Sauce	15
Mint Sauce	15
Yorkshire Pudding	16
Celery Sauce	16

Salads.
Chicken Salad	17
Lobster Salad	17
Sweet-bread Salad	18
Potato Salad	18
Ham Salad	18
Chicken Salad Dressing	18
Mayonnaise Dressing	19
Prepared Mustard	19

Meats, Poultry, &c.
To Corn Beef	19
Veal Pate	20
Veal Loaf	20
Veal Cutlets	20
Sausage Meat	20
Chicken Pudding	21
A very nice way to Cook Chicken	21
Chicken Croquetts, No. 1	21
Chicken Croquetts, No. 2	21
Old Fashioned Pot-pie	22
Beef Alamode	22
A Nice Breakfast Relish	22
Chicken Pie	23
Beef Bouille	23
Rolled Beef Steak	23
Hash	24
French Hash	24

Vegetables.
Egg Plant	24
Corn Oysters. No. 1	24
Corn Oysters, No. 2	25
Green Corn Pudding	25
Saratoga Potatoes	25
Corn Pudding	25
Salsify	26
Salsify, boiled	26
Sour Beans	26
Cold Slaw	26
Cold Slaw	27
Spinach	27
Macaroni	27
Stuffed Tomatoes	27
To Stew Tomatoes	27
Onions	28
Beets	28

New Potatoes ... 28
Mashed Potatoes ... 28
Green Peas ... 28
Cauliflower ... 29
Squashes ... 29
Winter Squash ... 29
Parsnips ... 29
Turnips ... 29
Lettuce ... 29
Boiled Hominy ... 29
Fried Hominy ... 30
Small Hominy ... 30
To Boil Rice ... 30
Fried Apples ... 30
Macaroni without cheese ... 30
Savory Cabbage ... 31
A Good Way to Cook Onions ... 31

Pickles and Catsups.

Rough and Ready Pickle ... 31
Cucumber Pickle, (3) ... 32
Red Cabbage and Cauliflower ... 32
Tomato Pickle ... 33
Cucumber Pickle, extra nice ... 33
Stuffing for Cucumber Mangoes ... 33
Tomato Catsup ... 34
Tomato Catsup, splendid ... 34
Tomato Sauce ... 34
Chow Chow ... 35
Mixed Pickle ... 35
Chili Sauce ... 35
Spiced Peaches and Plums ... 35
Peach Mangoes ... 36
Spiced Gooseberries ... 36
Chow Chow ... 36
Onion Pickles ... 37
Mangoes ... 37
White Walnuts ... 37
East India Pickle ... 37
Watermelon, Sweet Pickle ... 38
Higdon Pickle ... 38

Bread and Biscuit.

Yeast, (2) ... 39
French Rolls ... 39
Raised Biscuits ... 40
Biscuit ... 40
Maryland Biscuit (2) ... 40
Cream Biscuit ... 41
Sponge Biscuit ... 41
Bread ... 41
Parker House Rolls ... 41
Puffs ... 41

Pocket Rolls ... 42
Indian Meal Rolls ... 42
Brown Flour Rolls ... 42
Soda Biscuit, No. 1 ... 42
Soda Biscuit No. 2 ... 42
Indian Corn Biscuit ... 43
Rusk ... 43
Bread Cakes ... 43
Muffins, No. 1 ... 43
Muffins, No. 2 ... 43
Rice and Flour Muffins ... 44
Corn Muffins ... 44
Sally Lunn ... 44
Sally Lunn, very fine ... 44
Waffles ... 44
Rice Waffles ... 45
Drop Cakes ... 45
Corn Meal Batter Cakes ... 45
Corn Bread ... 45
Corn Cakes ... 45
Cream Cakes ... 46
Flannel Cakes ... 46
Brown Flour Mush ... 46
Gems ... 46
Diamonds ... 46
Graham Biscuit ... 47
Brown Bread ... 47
Boston Brown Bread ... 47
Graham Cup Cake ... 47

Pies, Puddings and Desserts.

Puff Paste ... 48
Lemon Pie, No. 1 ... 48
Lemon Pie, No. 2 ... 48
Mince Meat, extra ... 49
Mince Meat ... 49
Apple Custard Pie ... 49
Potato Pie ... 49
Pumpkin Pie ... 50
Cocoanut Pie, (2) ... 50
Marlborough Pie ... 50
Dauphines ... 51
Indian Pudding ... 51
English Pudding ... 51
Lemon Pudding ... 51
Queen of Puddings ... 51
Cottage Pudding ... 52
Brown Betty Pudding ... 52
Bread Pudding ... 52
Minute Pudding ... 53
Tapioca Pudding ... 53
Apple with Tapioca ... 53
Chocolate Pudding ... 53

CONTENTS.

Apple Meringue, (2)	53
Snow Pudding	54
Suet Pudding	54
Plum Pudding	54
Plum Pudding, baked	55
Plum Pudding	55
Strawberry Short Cake	56
Bevivo	56
Rice Meringue	56
Spanish Cream	56
Bohemian Cream	57
Charlotte Russe	57
Omelet Souffle	58
Rice Balls	58
Apple Custard	58
Fritters	58
Pound Pudding	59
Baked Flour Pudding	59
Boiled Custard	59
Puff Pudding	59
Cocoanut Pudding	60
Orange Pie	60
Wigwam	60
Lemon Custard	60
Ambrosia	61
Rice Pudding	61
Bombay Pudding	61
Dutch Blanc-Mange	61
Cocoanut Blanc-Mange	61
Fruit Meringue	62
Corn Starch Pudding	62
Fuller Pudding	62
Almond Custard	62
Syllabub	63
Ice Cream	63
Lemon Ice	63

Pudding Sauce.

No. 1	63
No. 2	64
No. 3	64
No. 4	64
No. 5, cold sauce	64
No. 6	64
No. 7	64
No. 8	64
Brandy Sauce, hard	64
Pudding Sauce	65

Cakes.

Fruit Cake	65
Fruit Cake, common	65
Black Cake	65

Washington Cake	66
Carolina Cake	66
White Cake	66
White Mountain Cake	66
Bride's Cake	67
Raisin Cake	67
Golden Cake	67
Silver Cake	67
Chocolate Cake	67
Cocoanut Cake	68
Lemon Cake	68
Almond Cake	68
Pound Cake, No. 1	68
Pound Cake, No. 2	68
Sponge Cake	69
Bread Cake	69
Cookies, (2)	69
Cup Cake, (2)	69
Currant Cake	70
Cream Cake	70
Buckeye Cake	70
Tea Cake, No. 1	70
Tea Cake, No. 2	70
Jumbles	71
Jumbles Almond	71
Macaroons	71
Almond Cake	71
Nut Cake	71
Rough and Ready Cake	71
Seed Cake	72
Gentleman's Ginger Bread	72
Scotch Cake	72
Lemon Mixture for Cake	72
Chicago Cake	73
Lancaster Cake	73
Ice Cream Cake	73
Kisses	73
Crullers, (3)	74
Doughnuts, (2)	74
Soft Ginger Bread, (2)	75
Ginger Snaps, (3)	75
Jelly Roll	76
Wafers	76
Marble Cake, (2)	76
Cream Cakes	77
Cocoanut Macaroons	77
Trifles	77
Cinnamon Wafers	77
Sand Tarts	77
Mrs. H's Jumbles	78
One Egg Cake	78
Mrs. Taylor's Ginger Cake	78
Sugar Ginger Bread	78

Icing.

Icing for Cake	78
Boiled Icing	79
Cold Icing	79
Icing	79

Jellies, Cordials, Wines, Preserves, &c.

Wine Jelly	79
Orange Jelly	80
Brandy Peaches	80
Brandy Peaches	81
Peach Marmalade	81
Blackberry Cordial	81
Cherry Cordial	81
Blackberry Syrup	81
Current Wine	82
Blackberry Wine	82
Raspberry Vinegar, (2)	82
Strawberry Vinegar	83
To Preserve Lemons	83
Conserve Peaches	83
Blackberry Jam	84
To make Jelly of any kind quickly	84
Orange Jelly	84
Canned Peaches	84
Pineapple Preserves	85
Cranberry Jelly	85

Drinks.

Coffee	85
Tea	86
Chocolate	86

Dishes For Invalids.

Beef Tea	86
Essence of Beef	87
Mutton Tea	87
Chicken Broth	87
Vegetable Broth	87
Panada	88
Boiled Flour	88
Toast Water	88
Mulled Wine	88
Caudle	89
Gruel	89
Oat Meal	89
Bran	89

Medical.

Remedy for Diphtheria	89
Remedy for Hoarseness or Loss of Voice	90
For Chronic Diarrhea	90
Splendid Remedy for Dysentery	90
Cure for Epilepsy	90
New Treatment for Cancer	91
Remedy for Toothache	91
Cholera Mixture	91
Sore Throat	91
Neuralgia	92
Milk as a Remedy	92
Treatment in Scarlet Fever	93
Receipt for Paregoric	93
To Cure Chills and Fever	93
To Break up a Cold	93
Sovereign Remedy for Ear-ache	94
Pepper Tea	94
Remedy for a Cough	94
Remedy for Rheumatism	94
Oranges as a Medicine	94
To make a Mustard Plaster	95
Treatment of Croup	95
Children's Sore Mouth	95
Another Remedy for Scarlet Fever	96

Miscellaneous.

Whitman's Taffy	96
Taffy	97
Caromels, (3)	97
Mrs. H's Candy	97
Egg-Nogg, (2)	97
Roman Punch	98
Cottage Cheese	98
Soap	99
Soft Soap	99
Hard Soap	99
To make White Wash	99
To Remove Rust from Steel	99
To Clean Marble	99
To Clean Paint	100
Cure for Felons	100
To Remove Paint	100
To Clean Carpets	100
To Destroy Vermin	100
Gloss for Starch	100
Ammonia for House-cleaning	101
To Prevent Blue from Fading	101
Good way to Wash Black Calico	102
To Prevent Calico from Fading	102
To Preserve Eggs	102
Cement for Broken China	102
To Clean Bottles	102
Whitening the Hands	102
To Clean Marble	102

Cleaning Silks.....................103
To Clean Straw Matting............103

Hints to Young Ladies.

For the Teeth..........................104
An Indispensable Powder.........104
To keep the Hair in Crimp.........104
Powder for the Skin...................104
To Remove Freckles..................105
Preparation for Rough Skin.......105
Splendid Hair Tonic..................106
Simple and Harmless Hair Dye..106
Remedy for Corns.....................107
For Cutaneous Eruptions..........107
A Remedy for Moth or Hepatic Spots.....................108

Cologne, [2]............................108
Common Cologne....................108
Cold Cream.............................108

Receipts sent in too Late for Classification.

English Plum Pudding..............109
Tapioca Cream........................109
Boston Brown Bread................109
Mixed Bread............................109
Boiled Bread...........................110
Bridget Cake...........................110
Chocolate Ice..........................110
Frozen Peaches.......................111
Strawberry Ice Cream..............111
Liniment for Sprains................111

Valuable Hints on Matching Carpets,............................Advertising Pages,

LIST OF ADVERTISERS.

John Bonnet, Jeweler.
Joseph Burnett & Co., Flavoring Extracts.
Burrough & Co., Furniture.
Drs. W. J. & E. C. Chandler, Dentists.
George R. Clements, Family Groceries.
Mrs. J. K. Crumbaker, Millinery.
Dooley & Co., Celebrated Yeast Powders.
Samuel Ebert, Toys, Perambulators, &c.
J. A. Filler, Carpets, Oil Cloths, &c.
E. E. Fillmore & Co., Hardware.
John Galigher & Co., Hats, Caps and Furs.
W. A. Graham & Co., Drugs, Paints, Oils, &c.
Alexander Grant, Dry Goods and Carpets.
Howe Sewing Machine Co.
W. H. Hurd, Books, Stationery, &c.
Johnson & Abbot, Dry Goods.
Jones & Abbot, Stoves, Fire Fronts, &c.
McCann Bros. & Hazlett, Hats, Caps, Furs, & Singer Sewing Machines.
R. S. Mershon, Jeweler.
H. D. Munson & Sons, Music Dealers.
Drs. Scott & Patterson, Dentists.
H. M. Sedgwick, Photographer, "Smith's Art Studio,"
C. Stolzenbach, Crackers, Confectionery, &c.
James R. Vansant, Millinery.
J. D. Warner, Bee Hive Notion Store.
H. C. Ward, Family Groceries.
Zanesville Woolen Manufacturing Company.

THE ADVERTISEMENTS.

Not alone for the commercial advantage which may be derived, but because of a generous willingness to share the expense of publication, have so many of the representative business men of Zanesville made use of the pages of "THE HOUSEKEEPER'S FRIEND." Advertisements have only been solicited from those whose names are synonymous with honorable dealing.

It is scarcely necessary to add, that all may place entire confidence in the character of the advertisers, no less than in the quality of the goods here offered for sale; this indorsement applying equally to manufacturers at a distance with those of our own city.

J. W. B.

PURITY.   FULL WEIGHT.   FULL STRENGTH.

DOOLEY'S

STANDARD

YEAST POWDER.

No Housekeeper who desires light, sweet and nutritious cookery, should be without this excellent Baking Powder.

| FIRST MADE 1858. |

The original determination of the manufacturers of this Powder to make an article which should be, in every way, reliable and healthful, should be put up full weight, exactly as represented, and should be of standard strength, has never been deviated from notwithstanding the host of inferior powders with which the market has been flooded.

Ask your grocer for it; and do not be put off with other brands represented as good as Dooley's.

Dooley & Brother,

MANUFACTURERS,

NEW YORK.

CULINARY GOODS

FOR SALE BY

W. A. GRAHAM & CO.,

Druggists,

ZANESVILLE, - - OHIO.

Corn Starch,	Chocolate,	Pure Salad Oil,
Tapioca,	Gelatine,	Pure Cream Tartar,
Rice Flour,	Oat Meal,	English Soda,
Farina,	Irish Moss,	Spices.

WE call the attention of housekeepers to the above articles kept constantly in stock, and recommend them as the purest and freshest in the market. Knowing the large adulteration of Cream of Tartar, Baking Soda and Spices, we have taken special pains in the selection of these goods. Our Cream of Tartar and Baking Soda is perfectly pure, and will be found much cheaper and more reliable than the so-called baking powders which are largely adulterated with flour, starch, &c. Our spices are all ground expressly for our retail trade, and are full strength. Our long experience and the advantages gained by large purchases, enables us to supply our trade with the best goods in the market, at the lowest possible rates.

We ask special attention to a line of

CHOICE FLAVORING EXTRACTS,

which we are now manufacturing. Having sold them for the past year with success, we offer them to our trade, and guarantee them to be equal to Burnett's in strength and flavor, and much lower in price.

W. A. GRAHAM & CO.

Why is it?

That so many people suffer from protracted derangements of health, which have their unsuspected origin in the DENTAL ORGANS?

BECAUSE they fail to appreciate the importance of their teeth until decay, diseased gums, and consequent suffering impel them to. *DON'T NEGLECT YOUR TEETH.*

If you have lost your natural ones, have them replaced at once by ARTIFICIAL DENTURES. Your organization is imperfect without them. If your food be not thoroughly masticated it can not be properly assimilated, and hence produces general derangement of stomach and system.

DENTAL APHORISMS.

Always consult an experienced and skillful dentist.

Cheap Dentistry is the worst possible economy.

Experience and skill are the result of *time* and *labor*, and should receive a remuneration equivalent to their worth.

Remember there are *degrees* in skill, and *difference* in the *value* of materials.

The slightest appearance of decay should receive immediate attention.

Decay is insiduous, and often requires the careful examination of the dentist to detect it.

W. J. CHANDLER, D. D. S.   E. C. CHANDLER, D. D. S.

DRS. W. J. & E. C. CHANDLER,

Attend to all branches of the profession at their rooms,

No. 112 Main Street, ZANESVILLE, O.

JOHN M. BONNET,
DEALER IN
FINE WATCHES,

CLOCKS, JEWELRY AND SILVERWARE.

156 Main Street, Zanesville O.

Special attention given to Watch Repairing and Fine Engraving.

MATCHING CARPETS.
BY A CARPET SALESMAN.

The practice has become almost universal with carpet dealers, to cut and match their customer's carpets. In all the large cities, the labor of tacking down, has also been removed from the hands of the buyer; men being employed by carpet houses to do this special work.

There are times, however, when every housekeeper has more or

STEINWAY & KNABE
PIANOS,

Acknowledged to be the Leading First Class Pianos of the World, and are everywhere spoken of as the

Standard of Excellence.

VALLEY GEM PIANOS,

The best Pianos in the Market, at a Medium Price.

HAINES BROS' PIANOS,

Thoroughly Well Made and Durable, and many other Good Pianos can be seen at

MUNSON'S MUSIC STORE,

108 Main Street, - - - - Zanesville, Ohio.

And are for sale at the lowest prices, and on the easiest terms, either for cash, or on monthly or quarterly payments. Send for Catalogues and Price Lists, free to any address.

C. STOLZENBACH,

Manufacturer of all kinds of

Crackers, Bread, Cakes,

AND

CONFECTIONERY.

Also Wholesale Dealer in Fruits, Nuts, &c.

135 Main Street, ZANESVILLE, OHIO.

(MATCHING CARPETS, CONTINUED.)

less carpet fitting to do; and these hints are offered in the hope that the path of domestic life, will in this respect, be made smoother.

In the first place, no receipt can be given for cutting a carpet without waste, unless the figure be adapted to the size of the room. This is so true, that if you take the length of the room in inches, and divide it by the length of the figure (also expressed in inches) you can readily tell what the waste if any, will be.

To make this more intelligible, I will suppose your room is fifteen feet long. This, of course is one hundred and eighty inches.

E. E. FILLMORE & CO.
HARDWARE
ZANESVILLE, - - OHIO.

LADIES' FINE SCISSORS,
4, 4½, 5, 5½, and 6 inch.

BUTTONHOLE CUTTERS,

FINE POINTS, SNIPE PATTERN.

HOUSE SHEARS,
7, 8, 9 and 10 inch.

PLATED KNIVES, Medium.

IVORY HANDLE KNIVES, Medium.

HARD RUBBER HANDLE TABLE KNIVES,

Hard-Rubber Handle **TABLE KNIVES & FORKS,**
The most durable Handle ever invented.

FINE IVORY CARVERS AND FORKS,

RUBBER HANDLE CARVERS,

IVORY AND RUBBER HANDLE STEELS,

LADIES' POCKET KNIVES,
In Ivory, Shell and Pearl.

Very Fine Assortment of Medium **TABLE CUTLERY,**

Bath Brick, genuine imported, Sapolio, Hand Sapolio, Rising Sun Stove Polish, &c., &c.

E. E. FILLMORE & CO.

Large Head Carpet Tacks, Black and Tinned Carpet Leathers.

JNO. GALIGHER & CO.

WHOLESALE AND RETAIL DEALERS IN

HATS, CAPS, FURS,

Straw Goods and Gloves,

141 Main Street,

JNO. GALIGHER,
C. W. FLETCHER, }
ZANESVILLE, O.

1876. $2.50 PER DAY

ZANE HOUSE,

Cor. Main and Fifth Streets,

ZANESVILLE, OHIO.

Mrs. A. E. COOK, Proprietress.

JAMES R. VANSANT,

Wholesale and Retail Dealer in

MILLINERY GOODS,

NOTIONS, DRESS TRIMMINGS, &c.

154 Main St., Opp. Zane House, ZANESVILLE, O.

(MATCHING CARPETS, CONTINUED.)

The figure in your carpet (*i. e.* the distance from one point to the next similar point) is two and one-half feet, or thirty inches; this will go six times into one hundred and eighty of course leaving no remainder; consequently no waste. Had the figure of your carpet measured three and one-half feet you would by the same process have found that four times the length of the figure would lack twelve inches of being long enough, and five times the length of the figure would be thirty inches too long. As you cannot spoil your carpet by cutting it too short, you must stand the loss of two and one-half feet on each width of carpet, if you buy that pattern.

ALEX. GRANT,

Dry Goods.

DRESS GOODS. DOMESTICS.

WHITE GOODS. WOOLENS.

GLOVES.

GRANT GETS GOOD GOODS.

LACES. LINENS.

HOSIERY.

CLOAKS. CARPETS.

86 MAIN STREET, ZANESVILLE.

"BEE HIVE" STORE.

J. D. WARNER,

NOTIONS AND FANCY GOODS.

LADIES' AND GENTS' FURNISHING GOODS.

Constantly receiving the *Latest Novelties* in
Neck Ties, Collars and Cuffs, Fancy Jewelry, Hosiery, Gloves, &c.

Always in stock a large variety of Hamburg Embroideries, Threads, Braids, Fine Soaps, Perfumeries, Merino and Gauze Underwear, Fancy Worsteds, Canvas, &c., &c.

13 and 15 Fifth Street, Maginnis Block.

H. C. WARD,
Grocer & Provisioner,

Flower Pots, Fruit Jugs, &c.

15 South 3rd Street,

ZANESVILLE, O.

(MATCHING CARPETS, CONTINUED.)

It is very amusing to hear some people declare that they can *always* cut a carpet without waste, by simply cutting a piece off at the beginning; just as though the cutting off had'nt to be done with each succeeding strip. Waste is waste, whether it occur at the beginning or at the ending.

Where carpets have no "up and down," the rule is, to cut through the center of the figure. You can then reverse the roll and run back to the other end. If this first end has been cut through the center of the figure, you have no trouble even though the carpet contains a double figure.

C. H. SCOTT, D.D.S.   A. PATTERSON, Jr., D.D.S.

Drs. Scott & Patterson,
Dentists,

OVER ALEX. GRANT'S STORE.   ZANESVILLE, O.

ZANESVILLE CARPET HOUSE.

J. A. FILLER,
DEALER IN

Carpets, Oil Cloths, Mattings, Wall Papers, Window Shades,

&c., &c.

No. 56 Main Street,

W. H. CARY, *Salesman*.   ZANESVILLE, O.

BURROUGH & CO.

Manufacturers and Dealers in Every Variety of

PARLOR SUITS,

Chamber Sets, Dining Room Sets, Cabinet Ware, Chairs, &c.

No. 57 MAIN STREET,

ZANESVILLE, O.

NEWS, *Fine Stationery,* **FANCY GOODS,**
GO TO EBERT.

CROQUET from 98 cents to $10.
Children's Carriages, 60 different styles, from $8 to $50.

EBERT'S, Opposite Zane House.

BURNETT'S
Standard Extracts.
FOR COOKING PURPOSES.

"Pre-eminently superior."	Parker House,	Boston.
"The best in the world."	Fifth Avenue Hotel,	New York.
"Used exclusively for years."	Continental Hotel,	Philadelphia.
"We find them the best."	Southern Hotel,	St. Louis.
'We use them exclusively."	Sherman House,	Chicago.
"We find them excellent."	Occidental,	San Francisco

The superiority of these extracts consists in their perfect purity and great strength. They are warranted free from the poisonous oils and acids which enter into the composition of many of the factitious fruit flavors now in the market. They are not only true to their names, but are prepared from fruits of the best quality and are so highly concentrated that a comparatively small quantity only need be used.

MILLINERY EMPORIUM.

MRS. J. K. CRUMBAKER,
DEALER IN
Real and Imitation Laces,
Kid Gloves, Corsets, Parasols, &c.,

Nos. 36 & 110, Main Street,

ZANESVILLE, OHIO.

(MATCHING CARPETS, CONTINUED.)

In case the carpet *has* an "up and down" then you must begin each strip at precisely the same point, *unless*, the figures alternate, as in the case with almost all Brussels, Wilton, Axminster, and carpets of like grade. In case the figures *do* thus alternate, the plan is to cut from both ends of the roll, being careful to have the roll begin and end in different figures. For instance, you are cutting a Brussels carpet, containing a bunch of autumn leaves, and a group of pansies. It would be a violation of taste to have a row of the leaves straight across the room, and a row of the pansies. They should of course run diagonally. Consequently, if you have seven strips of carpets to cut, numbers 1, 3, 5 and 7, must begin with the leaves, and 2, 4 and 6 with the pansies.

173.
JOHNSON & ABBOT,

173 MAIN STREET,
ZANESVILLE, OHIO.

RETAIL DEALERS IN

DRESS GOODS,

Of the latest styles. Splendid Stock of **Black Silks**, also Shawls, Table Linens, Napkins, Towels, Curtain Nets, &c. Bleached and Unbleached Sheetings, all widths—4-4, 5-4. 6-4, 7-4, 8-4, 9-4, 10-4.

Buying our goods strictly for cash, we are enabled at all times to make the *Lowest Prices*. Everything marked in *Plain Figures*. Please look at our stock.

JOHNSON & ABBOT.

---

17 REASON'S WHY YOU SHOULD PURCHASE THE
HOWE SEWING MACHINE.

1. Beauty and excellence of stitch, alike on both sides of the fabric sewed.
2. Strength, beauty and durability of seam, that will neither rip nor ravel.
3. Complete control over both threads.
4. A perfectly uniform tension in the the shuttle, which does not vary from a full to an empty bobbin—an objection so common to other machines.
5. An automatic self-regulating take-up, that prevents missing of stitches in crossing heavy seams.
6. It contains the material for its own repair.
7. Sews equally well with any kind of thread.
8. It has less wearing points than any other.
9. A hemmer that will make any width of hem or fell.
10. Braiding the most complicated patterns, with any width or kind of braid.
11. A quilter that will adjust itself to any thickness of material.
12. Tucking any fabric without injury or pucker.
13. Sewing the finest fabric without injury or pucker, and the heaviest material with the greatest ease.
14. Compactness, simplicity and durability.
15. Ease of operation and management.
16. It draws up a stitch as it is drawn up by hand.
17. The presser foot is easily set out of the way when you set a needle or put under work.

THE HOWE MACHINE CO.
No. 110 Main Street, - - - ZANESVILLE, OHIO.

J. M. BRUNSON, Manager.

WILLIAM H. HURD,

BOOKSELLER,

STATIONER,

Binder and Job Printer,

Opposite Odd Fellows' Hall,

ZANESVILLE, OHIO.

(MATCHING CARPETS, CONTINUED.)

In cutting high-priced Carpets, something is often gained by taking off a width, and then a recess or corner piece ; and sometimes when the whole carpet must either be cut a few inches too short, or else a couple of feet too long, it will be found economical to border it. Indeed, it may safely be said that no carpet in neutral colors is complete without a border of blue, scarlet, crimson or green ; whichever may most elegantly harmonize with the furnishing of the room.

There will sometimes be met with in all collections of ingrain carpets, a pattern containing a third or intermediate figure, which, to be properly matched, requires that you should cut *between* the two principal figures. "There is no rule without an exception," and this is the only circumstance I know of in which it is safe to do otherwise than cut through the *center of a figure* in carpets having no "up and down."

McCann Bros. & Hazlett,

DEALERS IN

Hats, Caps, Furs,

VALISES,

AND LADIES' AND GENTS'

FURNISHING GOODS.

SIGN OF THE  BLACK BEAR.

THE LARGEST STOCK OF

UNDERWEAR

For LADIES, GENTS AND CHILDREN, of any house in the city.

White and Colored Shirts

ALWAYS ON HAND.

Special orders taken for shirts. A Full line of White and Fancy Hose and Half Hose. Scarfs, Mufflers, Ties, Bows, &c.

Agents for the Singer Sewing Machine.

No. 136 Main Street,   ZANESVILLE, OHIO.

ESTEY ORGANS,
AND
Mason and Hamlin Organs,

THE BEST IN THE WORLD,

Are sold by us at Wholesale and Retail. We also have in stock,

Burdette, Prince, Smith, Needham, Shoninger, New England, Taylor & Farley,

And other makes of Organs, which we can sell at lowest prices to those who prefer them to the Estey or Mason & Hamlin. Call and see the different styles and makes of

ORGANS.

Our Stock is now complete, and prices lower than ever. None sell lower. We sell Organs on monthly or quarterly rental payments. Every Instrument fully warranted.

Circulars and Price Lists free to any address.

H. D. MUNSON & SONS,
MUSIC DEALERS,
ZANESVILLE, OHIO.

GEO. R. CLEMENTS,
RETAIL GROCER

SPECIALTIES.

Fine Teas, strictly pure; Fine Roasted Coffees, a Complete Assortment of Canned Goods, Spices, Extracts and Fancy Goods.

17 South Third Street, - - *ZANESVILLE, OHIO.*

(MATCHING CARPETS, CONTINUED.)

Many persons imagine that a large figure is more wasteful than a small one. Not necessarily so. The figure may be five feet long—as is often the case in Tapestry Brussels—and if your room is seventeen and one-half feet, you are all right; because three and a half times the length of the figure will just fill the room. In cutting ingrains and 3-plys it is not necessary to allow anything for a narrow hem, as the elasticity of the carpet will be sufficient. I would recommend, however, to allow enough for a generous hem, as it is easier to drive a tack in this kind.

ZANESVILLE
Woolen Manufacturing Co.

If you want Woolen Goods that are made of WOOL, be sure to ask for those of our manufacture. We produce Flannels of all kinds; White and Colored, Plain and Plaid, Light and Heavy.

FLANNELS,

YARNS.   **JEANS.**

TRADE Z MARK.

CASSIMERES.

Our Yarns are full cut and full count, of every color and combination, all shades in Jeans, and styles in Cassimeres. Not a particle of shoddy or hair enters into the composition of our goods. Since

"The Best are always the Cheapest,"

the buyer will practice true economy, by using our goods.

See that our trade mark is on every label, and ask for **Zanesville Woolens.**

Kept by all First-Class Stores.

Smith's Art Studio,

No. 101 Main Street, - - - ZANESVILLE, OHIO.

FINE PHOTOGRAPHS, ANY SIZE,

PORTRAITS IN INDIA INK

AND
WATER COLORS,
FROM
LIFE OR OLD PICTURES.

Especial Attention Given to Making Childrens' Pictures.

All Work Guaranteed Satisfactory.

H. M. SEDGWICK,
OPERATOR.

USE
JOSEPH BURNETT & CO'S
WORLD RENOWNED
Flavoring Extracts.

SEE PREVIOUS ADVERTISEMENT.

(MATCHING CARPETS, CONCLUDED.)

There remains only to point out a sort of chronic mismatch in Tapestry Brussels. I refer to that occasioned by the mechanical inaccuracy of the colors. For lack of a better name I call it the "wolf." Manufacturers have labored for years to overcome this obstacle, but with varying success. If you have a width showing the "wolf" pretty badly, turn it over and dampen the wrong side. This will shrink the linen back—flax and hemp being susceptible to moisture—and will be found sufficient as a general thing. Do not pucker the seams of such a carpet in the vain hope that the "puckers" will tramp out, for they won't. Better make a compromise in the pattern.

Ralph S. Mershon,

DEALER IN

WATCHES,

Diamonds, Rich Jewelry,

AND

GOLD CHAIN.

Sterling Silver AND **Silver Plated** GOODS,

SUITABLE FOR

Anniversary and Bridal Gifts.

Special Attention Given to

DESIGNING AND ENGRAVING
MONOGRAMS.

Odd Fellows' Building,

Zanesville, Ohio.

Jones & Abbot,
ZANESVILLE, OHIO.

Third Street Foundry.

www.ingramcontent.com/pod-product-compliance
Lightning Source LLC
Chambersburg PA
CBHW030247170426
43202CB00009B/662